T0089244

My Big American Road Trip Coloring Book

BuzzPop

Connect the dots to see what you'll be driving in!

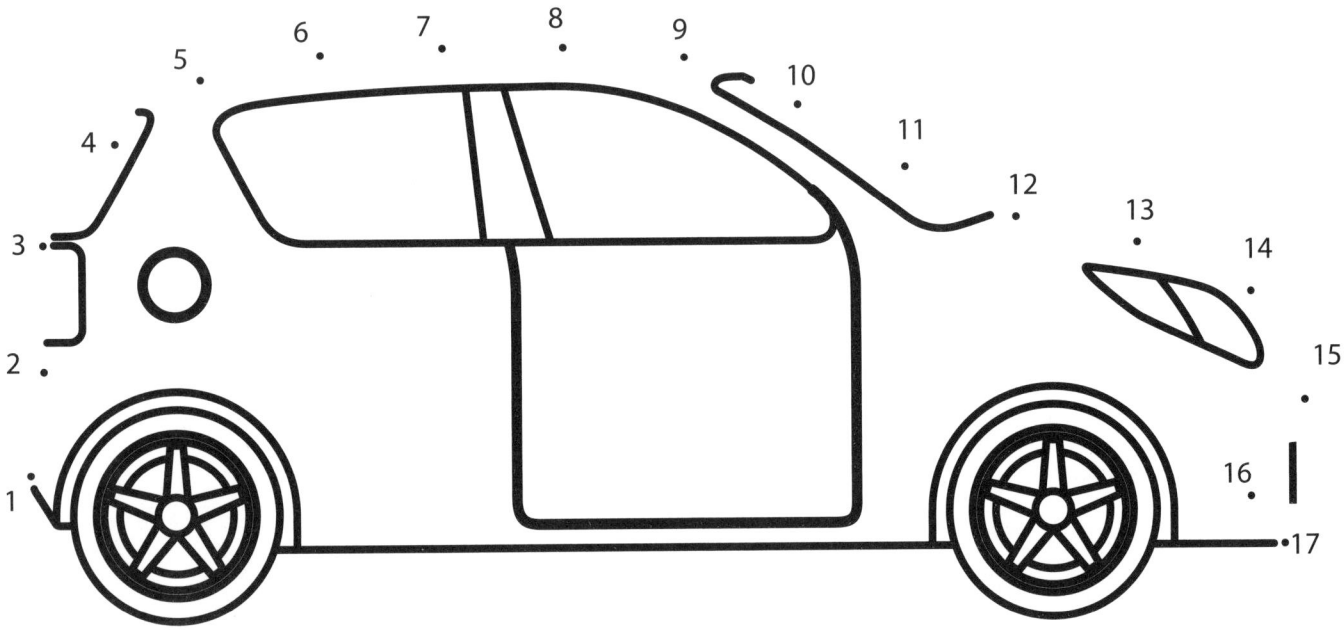

Make sure to pack plenty of snacks for the ride!

What else will you bring with you?

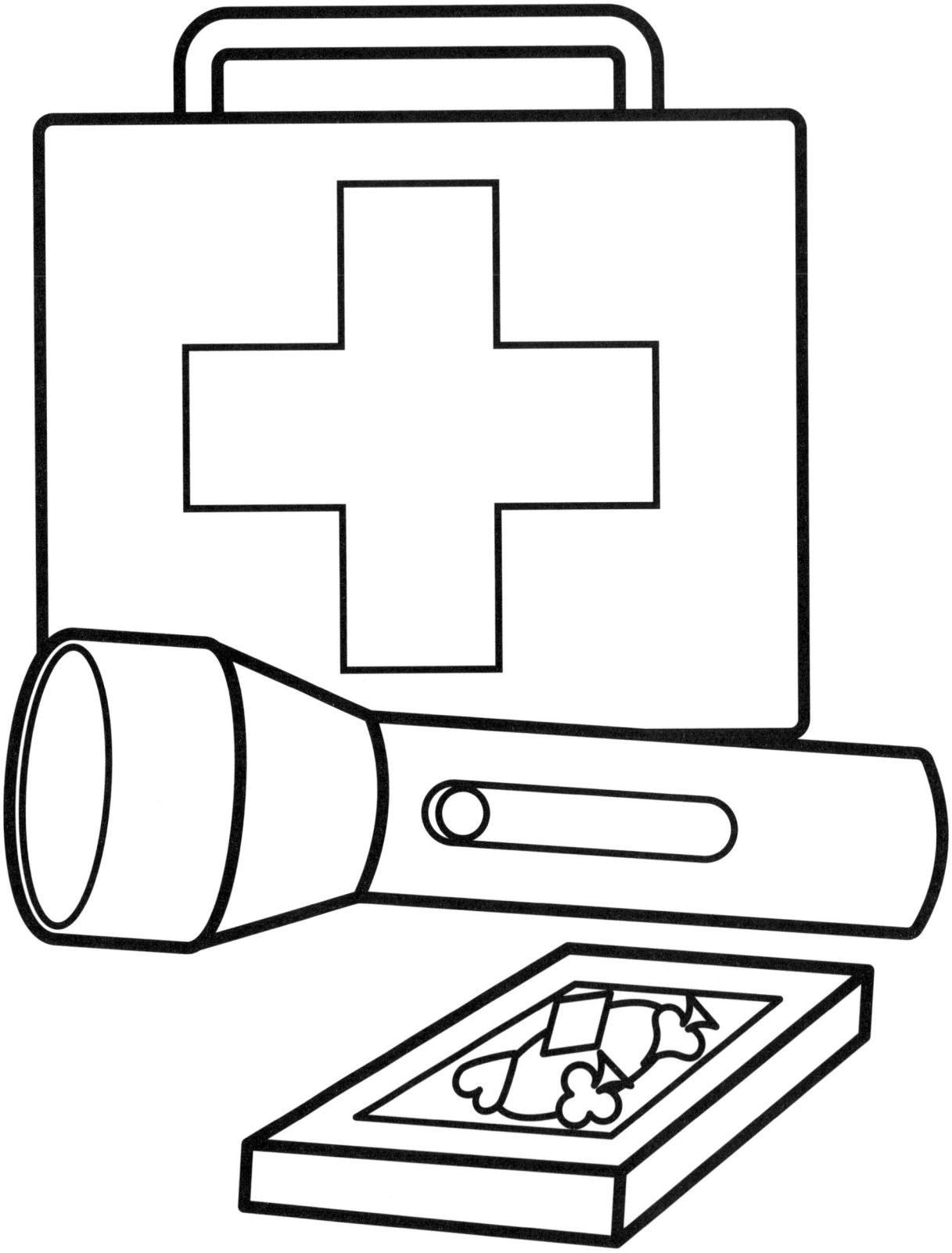

This map will help you get to your destination!

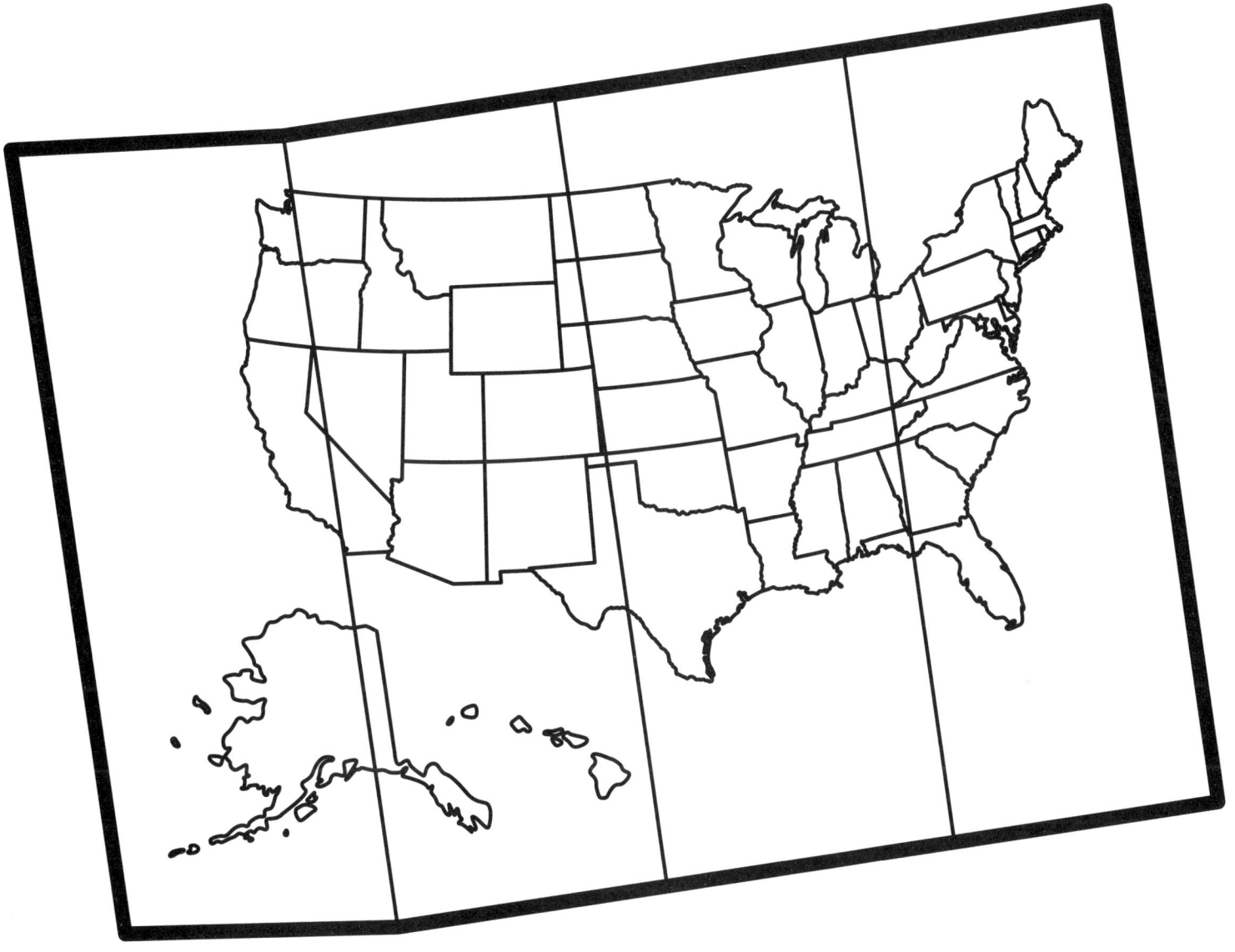

And now we're off on a big adventure!
Fill in the sign with your home state or town.

Binoculars help you spot things that are far away!

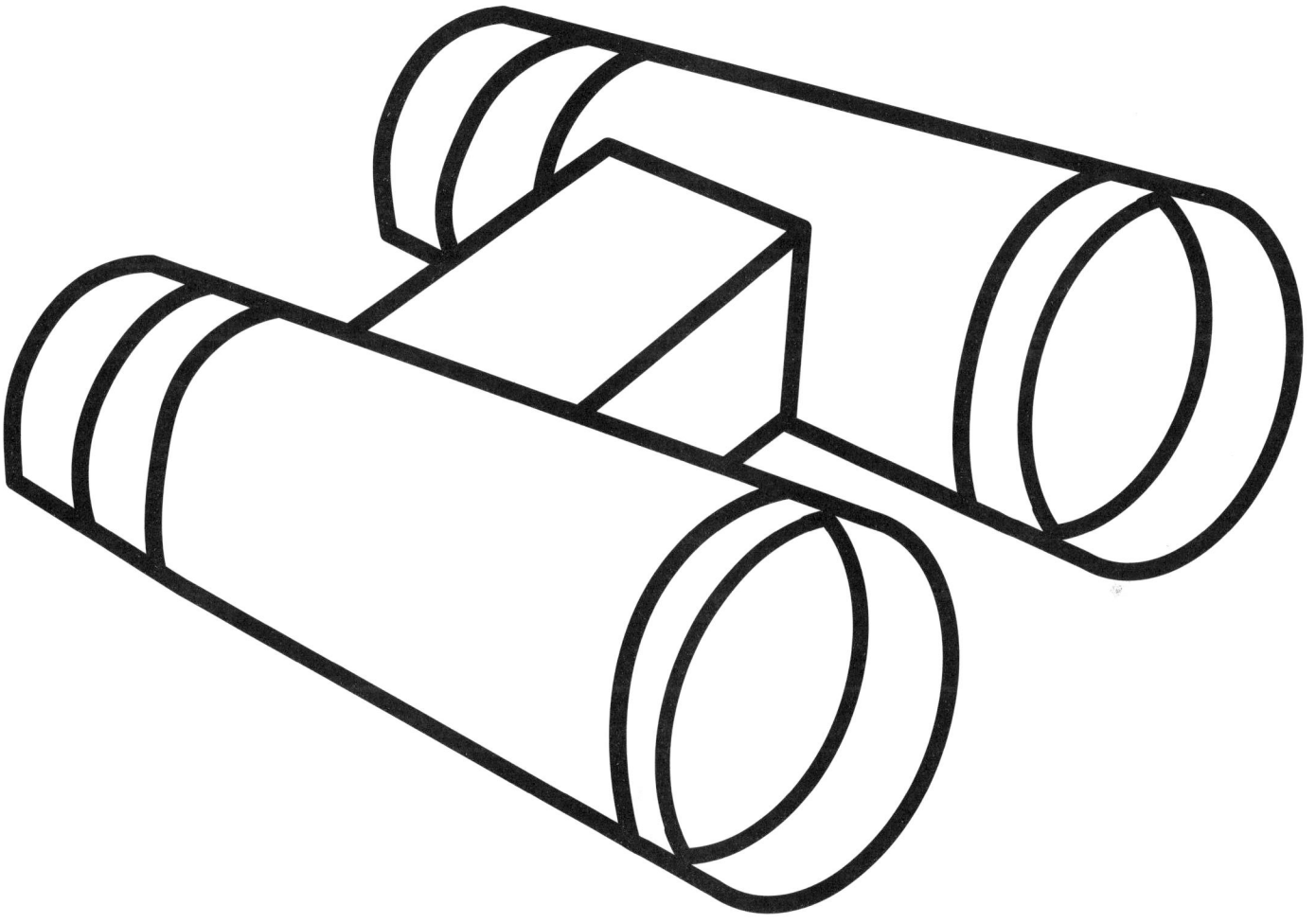

This black bear is off to find a snack!

Did you know bears eat fruit, nuts, and plants?

Wolves live in the wilderness across America!
Circle the wolf that is different from the others.

Draw what you would see out of the car window!

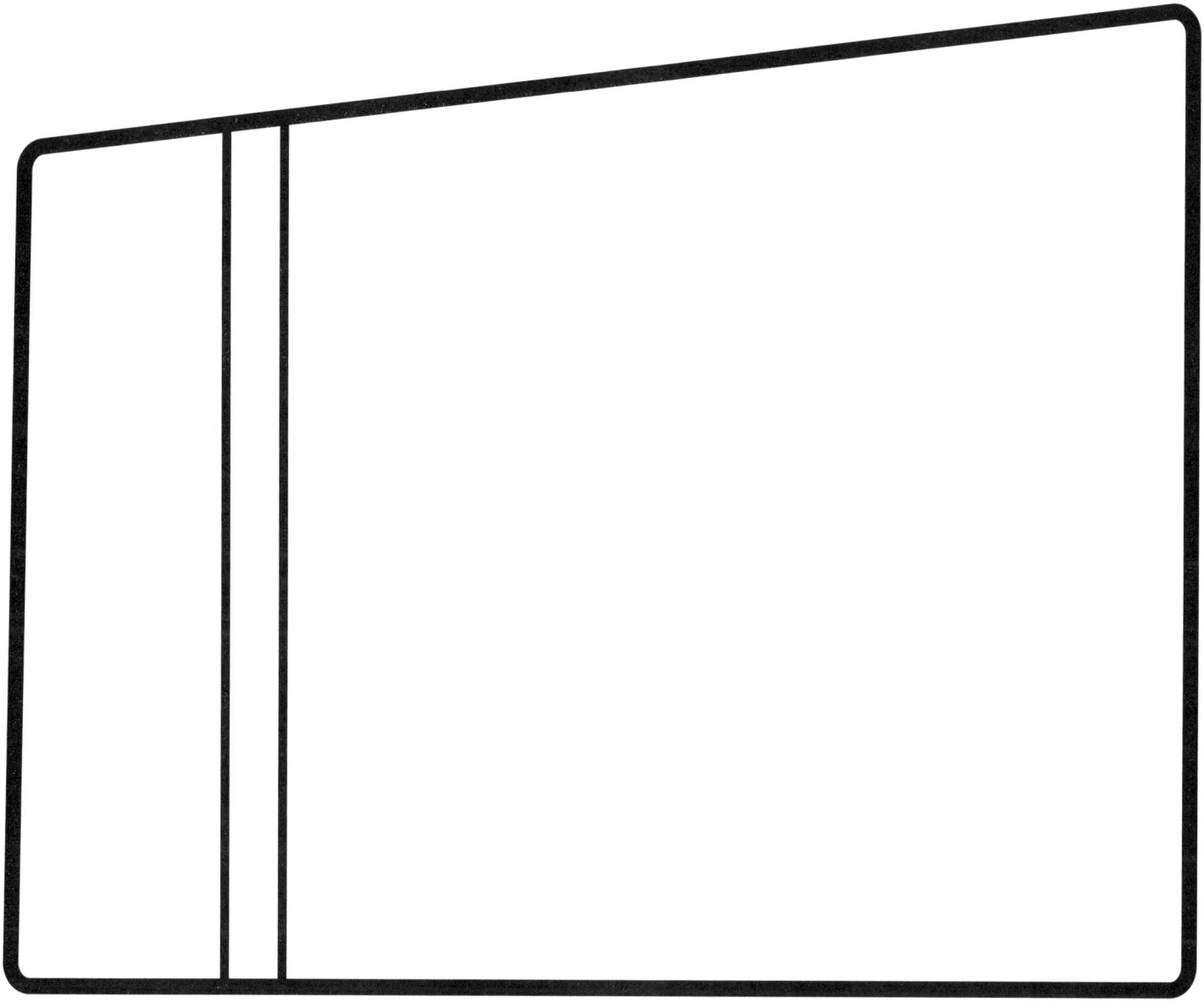

Wrigley Field is a famous baseball park!

What equipment do you need to play baseball?

Cloud Gate is known to many as "the bean" and is located in Millennium Park in Chicago!

Did you know that the cardinal is the state bird of Illinois?

We are now passing through a town called Santa Claus! It's in Indiana.

Peony plants can live to be 100 years old!

Did you know that horses can sleep lying down or standing up?

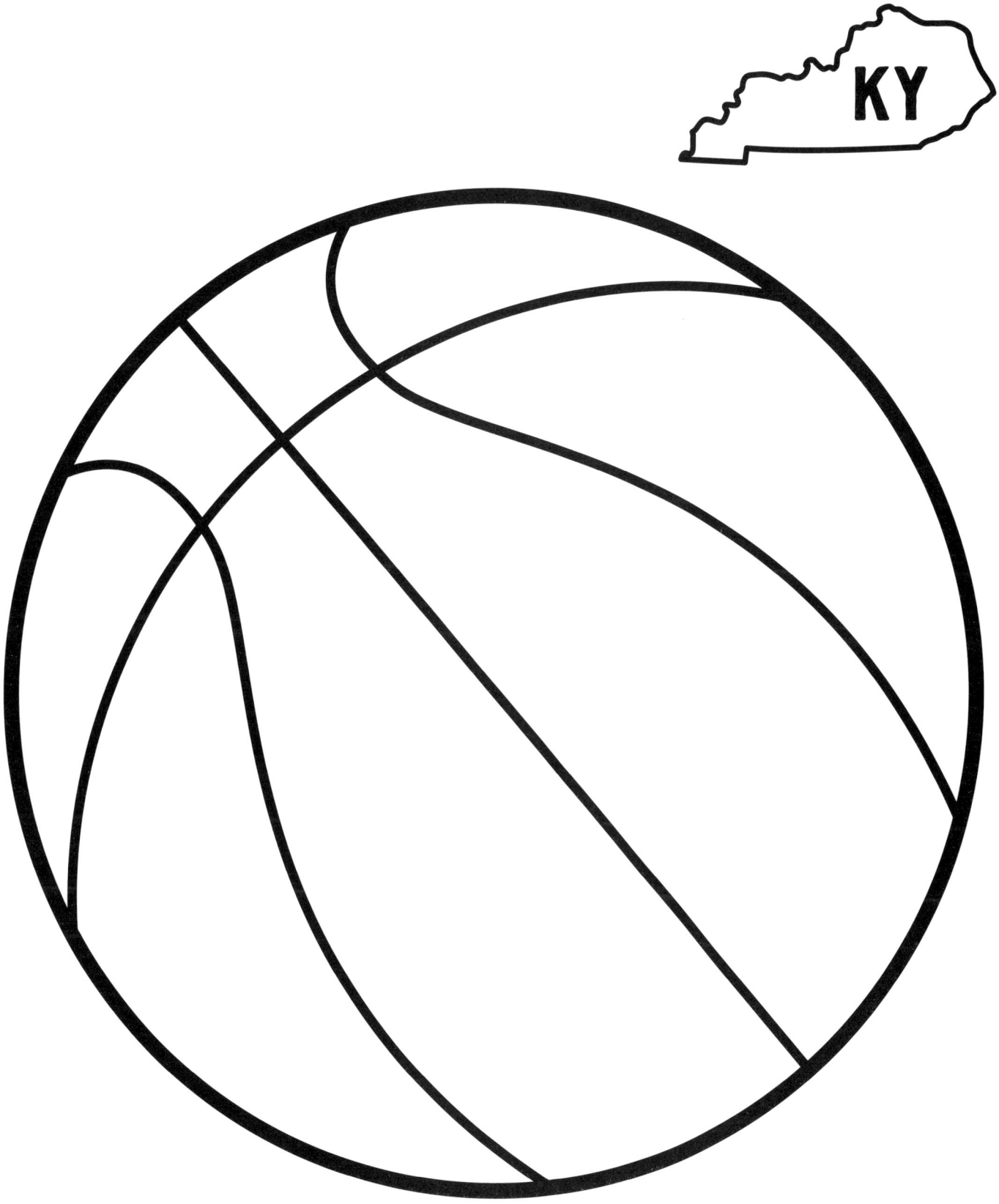

Kentucky is famous for college basketball!

Connect the dots to reveal a tasty snack!

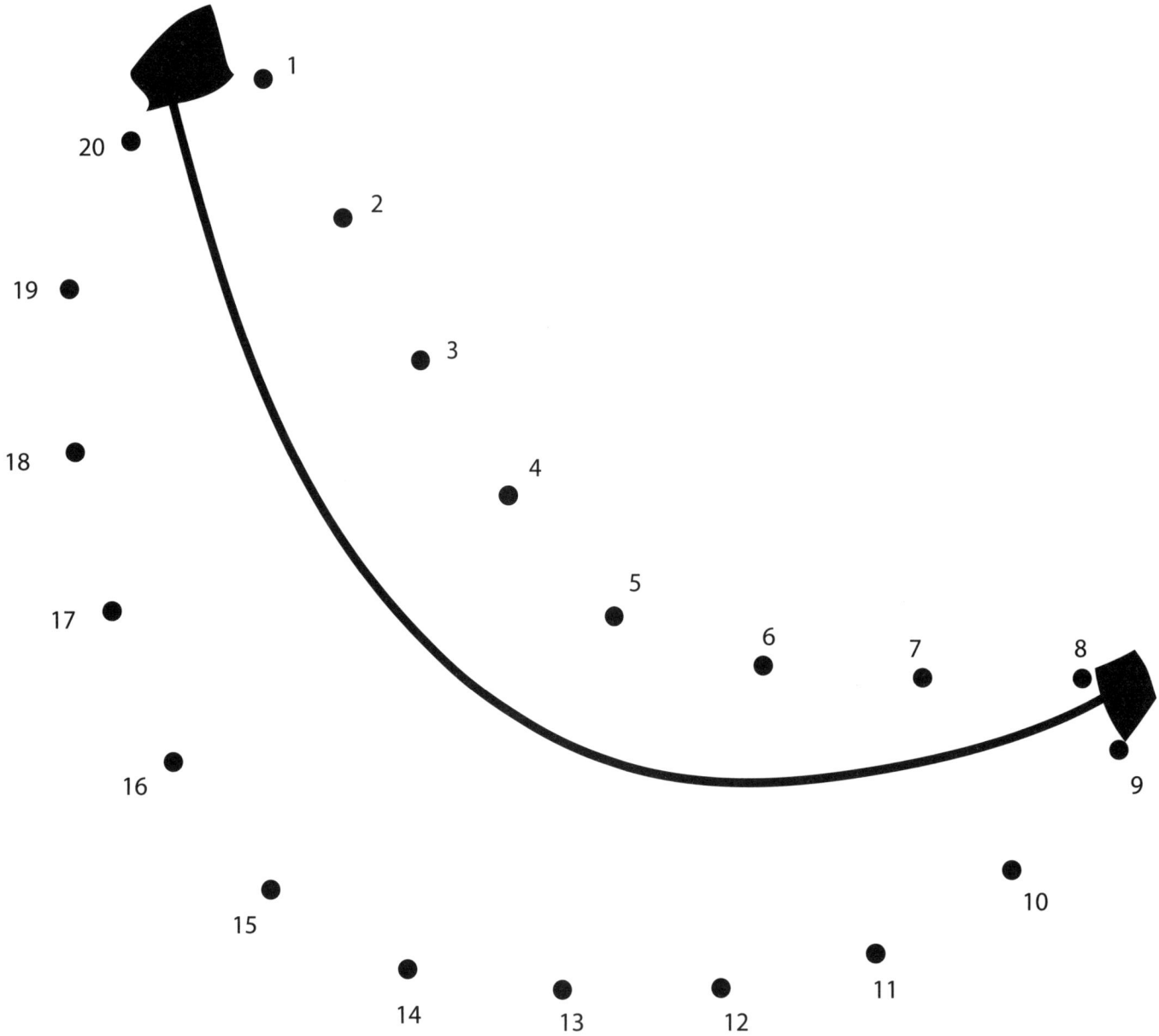

Carnations are Ohio's official state flower!

Let's rock!
Ohio has the Rock & Roll Hall of Fame.

Hop! Hop! Hop! Did you know baby rabbits are called "kittens"?

Botanical gardens are a great place to view and learn about plants!

Does this remind you of a vegetable? It's an island off the shore of Michigan in Lake Huron. It's called Turnip Rock!

Robins are Michigan's state bird!

Lake Champlain sits among Vermont, New York, and Canada!

There may be a monster lurking in Lake Champlain.
Locals call him Champ!

How many fish do you spot in this river?
Your answer:_____

Vermont is famous for its ice cream!
What's your favorite flavor?

Can you match each animal to its name?

Wolf

Moose

Bear

Farmers' markets are a great way to support local farms!

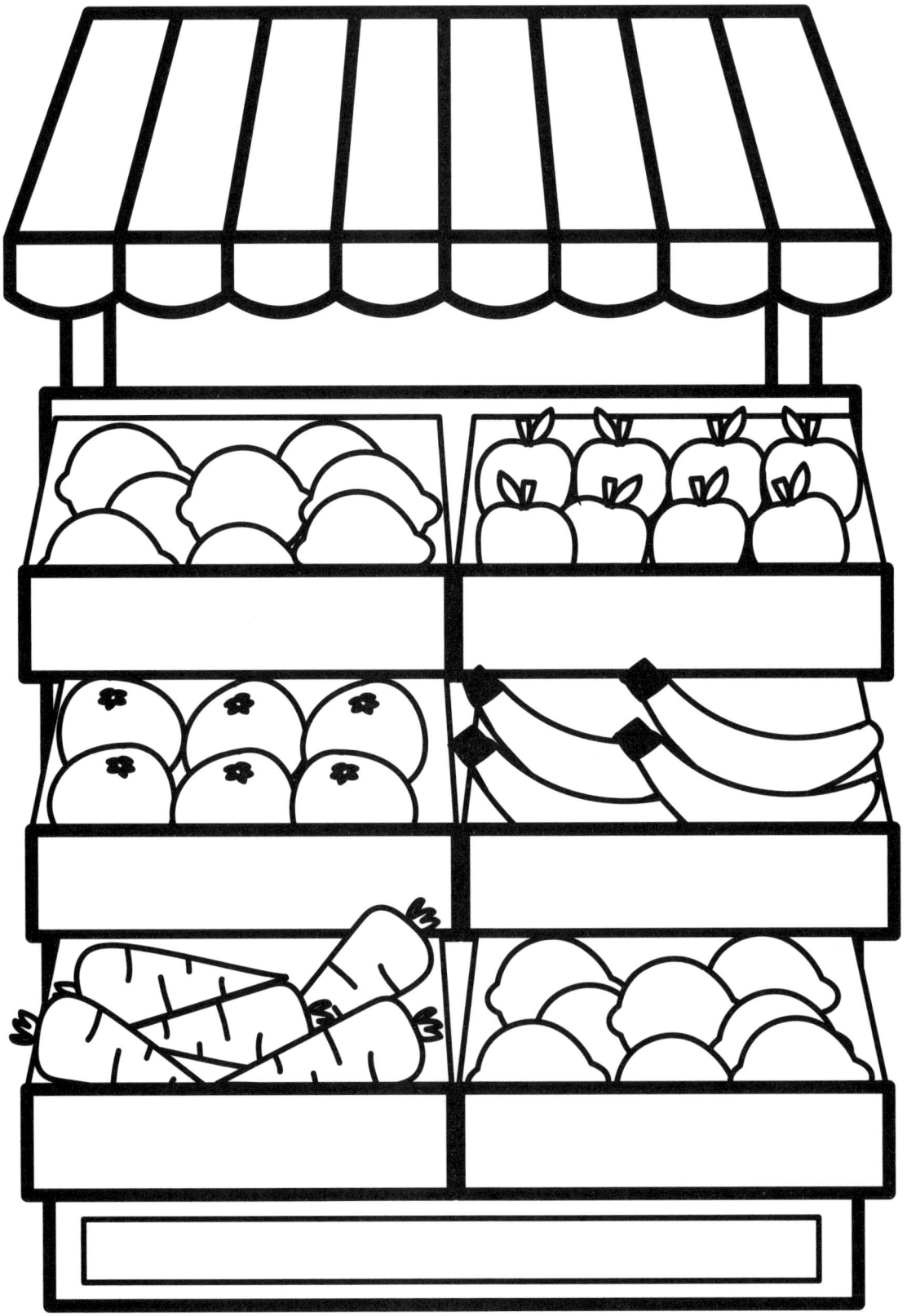

Moose antlers can reach up to six feet end to end!

How about taking the Cog way to
the summit of Mount Washington?
It's one of New Hampshire's greatest attractions!

Bobcats can run up to 30 miles per hour, but they prefer walking!

The purple lilac is the official state flower of New Hampshire!

Help the beaver get back to its dam!

It's a great day for a ferry ride!

Welcome to Acadia National Park!

Did you know that Maine's state flower is a white pine cone, even though it isn't actually a flower?

Maine is known for lobsters!

Maine is home to the world's largest rotating globe!
It's called Eartha.

Mount Katahdin is the highest mountain in Maine and at the end of the Appalachian Trail!

Racoons are nocturnal, meaning they're only active at night!

Can you match each snack to its name?

Chips

Popcorn

Apple

Boston is home to America's first lighthouse!

Whale watching is fun!
This is a humpback whale.

Draw your own dinosaur!

That's a dinosaur footprint! Did you know that there are hundreds of dinosaur tracks along the Connecticut River?

We're now passing through Cape Cod.
Keep your eye out for Salty the Seahorse.
He's 38 feet tall!

Did you know that opossums have great memory?

Sample some chowder recipes and help determine who has the best chowder in New England!

A traditional clambake includes corn on the cob, potatoes, clams, and lobster.

Did you know that lobsters shed their shells each year and grow a new one?

Roar!
The Philadelphia Zoo is the oldest zoo in the U.S.

The Liberty Bell is a symbol of freedom.
It's one of America's biggest attractions!

Wow! Niagara Falls sure is beautiful!

New York's nicknamed the Big Apple!
What's your nickname?

The Empire State Building has 102 floors!

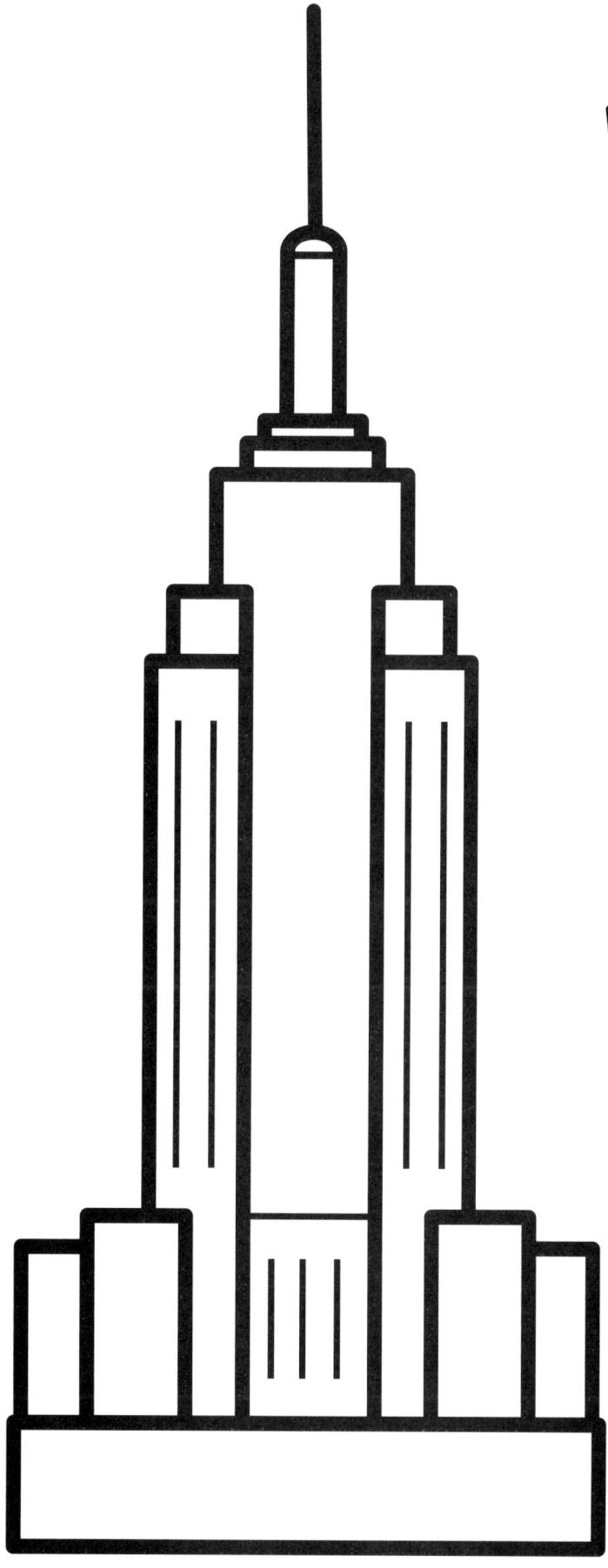

There are a lot of pigeons in New York City!

New York is a great place to see a play or a show!

Oh, look. There's the Statue of Liberty!

Did you know New York's state flower is the rose?

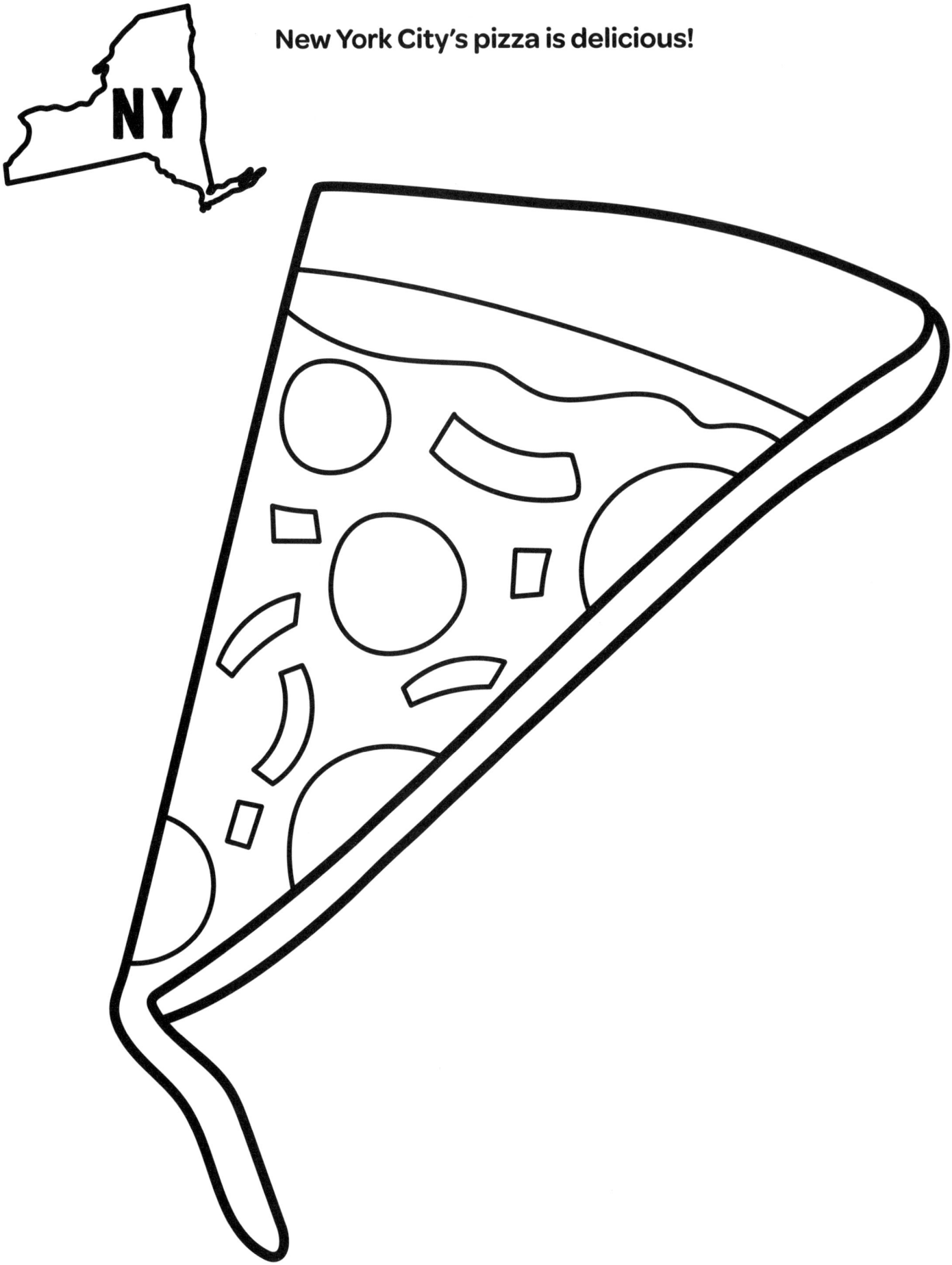

New York City's pizza is delicious!

New Jersey is also known as the Garden State thanks to its farmers!

Let's go down the shore!

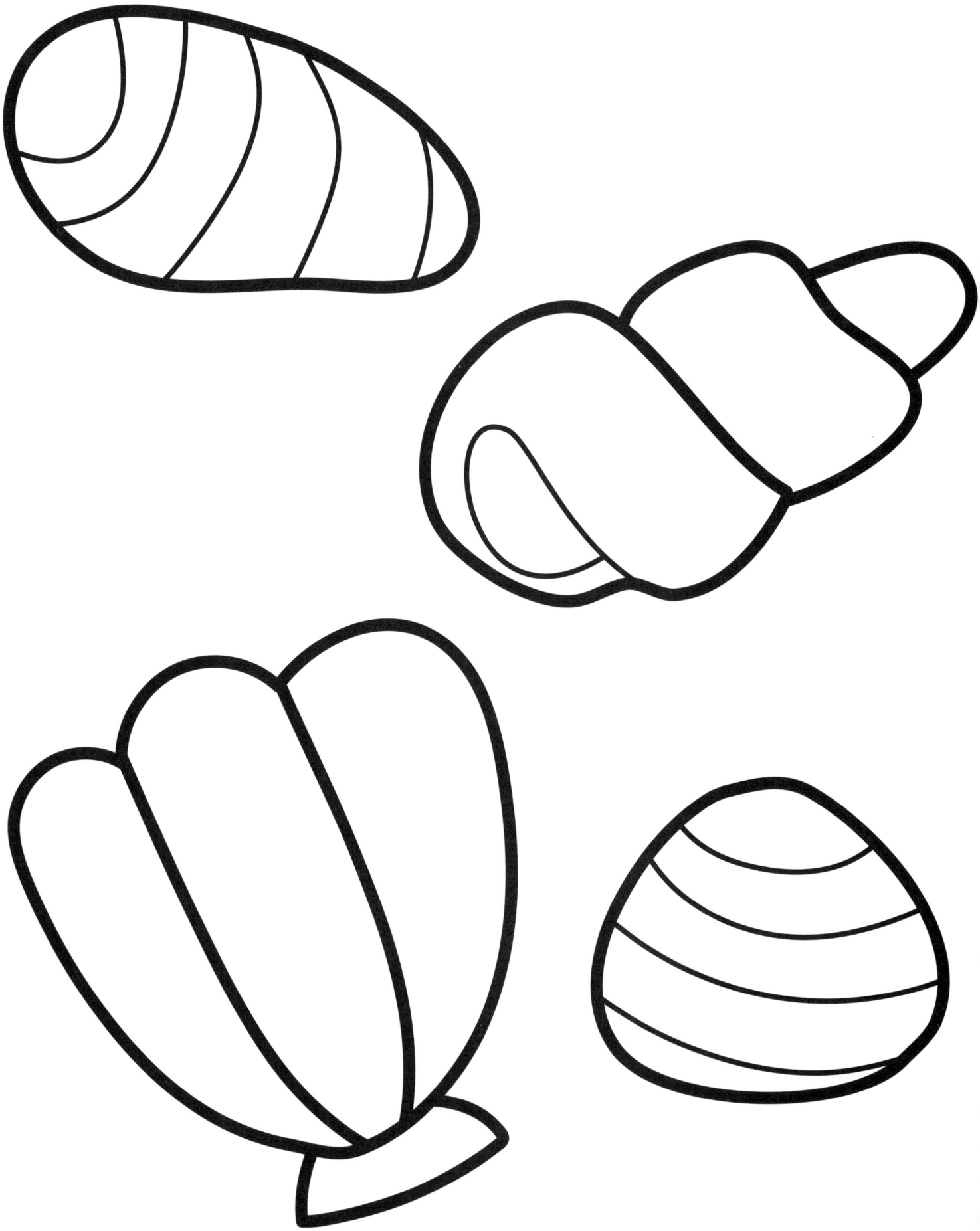

Decorate this sandcastle!

Let's check out some arcade games!

Atlantic City has a popular boardwalk.
NJ

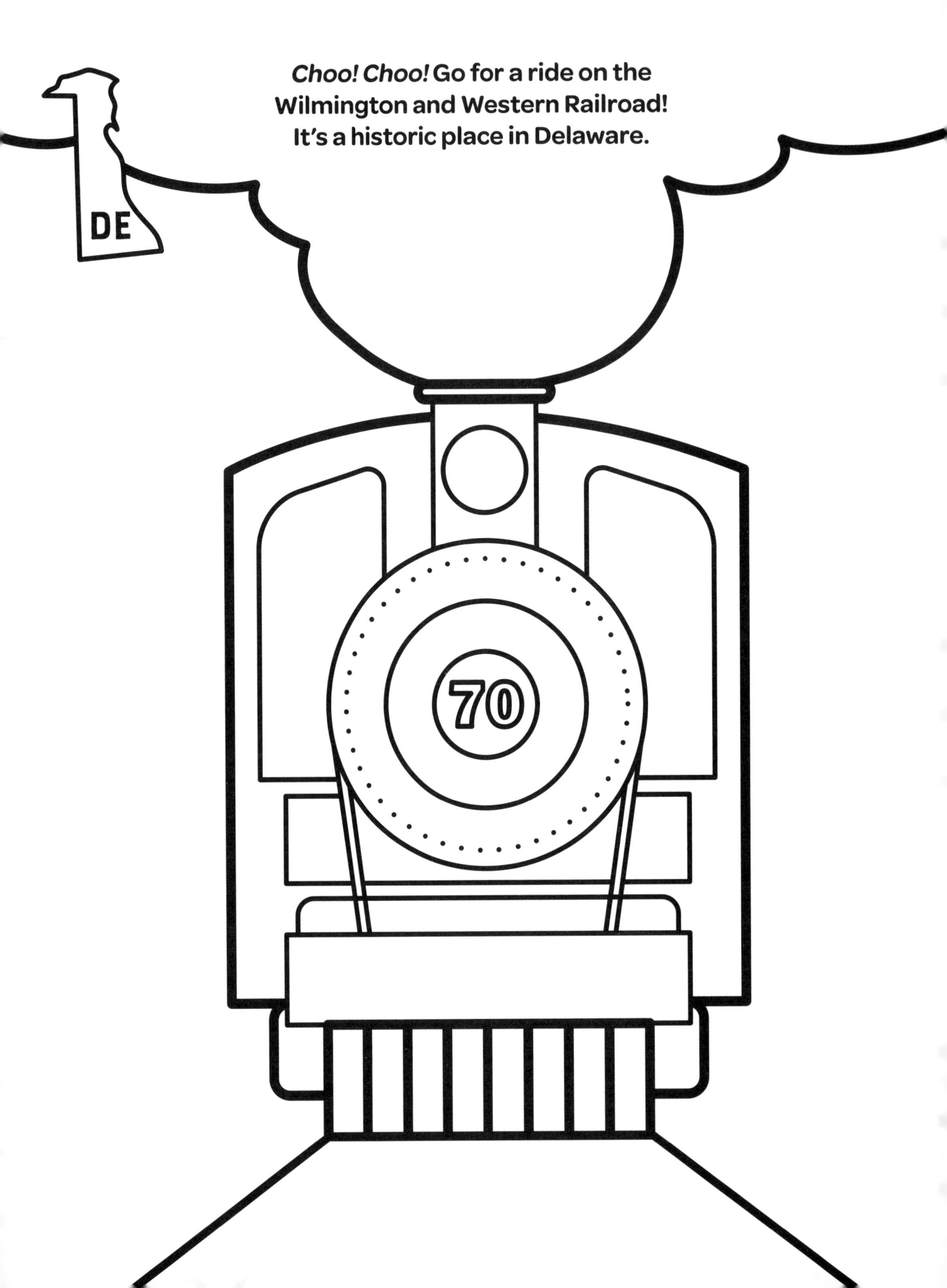

Choo! Choo! Go for a ride on the Wilmington and Western Railroad! It's a historic place in Delaware.

We're back on the road! What's your favorite music to listen to?

The Baltimore oriole is Maryland's state bird!

Maryland is known for its blue crabs found in Chesapeake Bay.

We're passing the U.S. Capitol.
Your voice and vote matters!

About six million people visit the Lincoln Memorial every year!

Oak trees are one of the oldest trees on the planet.
They can live up to 1,000 years!

The New River Gorge Bridge is the third-longest single arch bridge in the world!

Let's float down the river in an inner tube. Don't forget your life vest!

The Shenandoah Valley in Virginia is nicknamed "The Big Valley."

Horses are roaming the fields in the Great Smoky Mountains!
This forest is on the border of Tennessee and North Carolina.

Did you know there are eleven types of herons that can be found in both North and South Carolina?

River otters live in rivers, marshes, and ponds, making South Carolina's coast a great home!

The Georgia Aquarium is the largest in the world!
What's your favorite sea creature?

The trees on Driftwood Beach are beautiful.

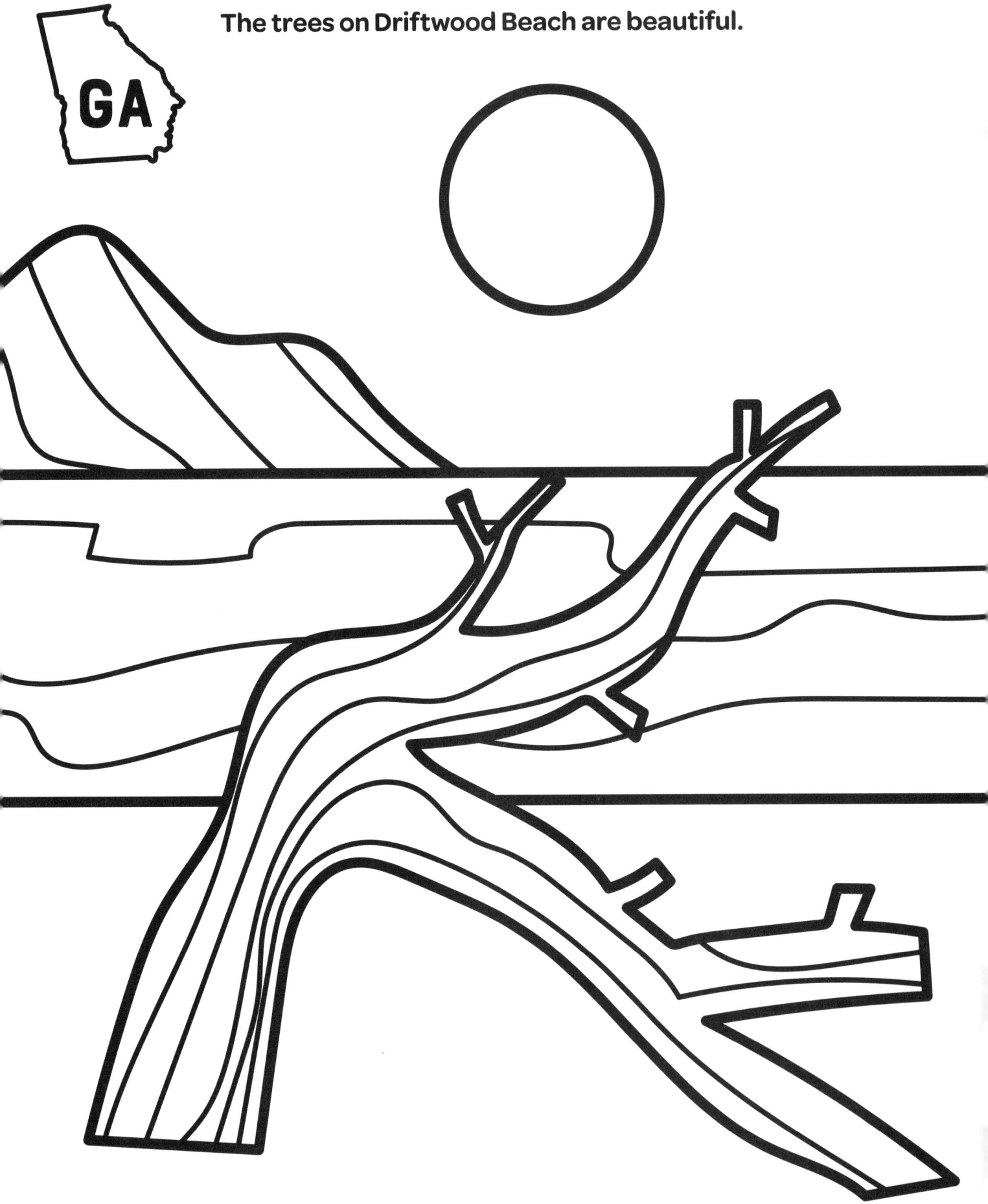

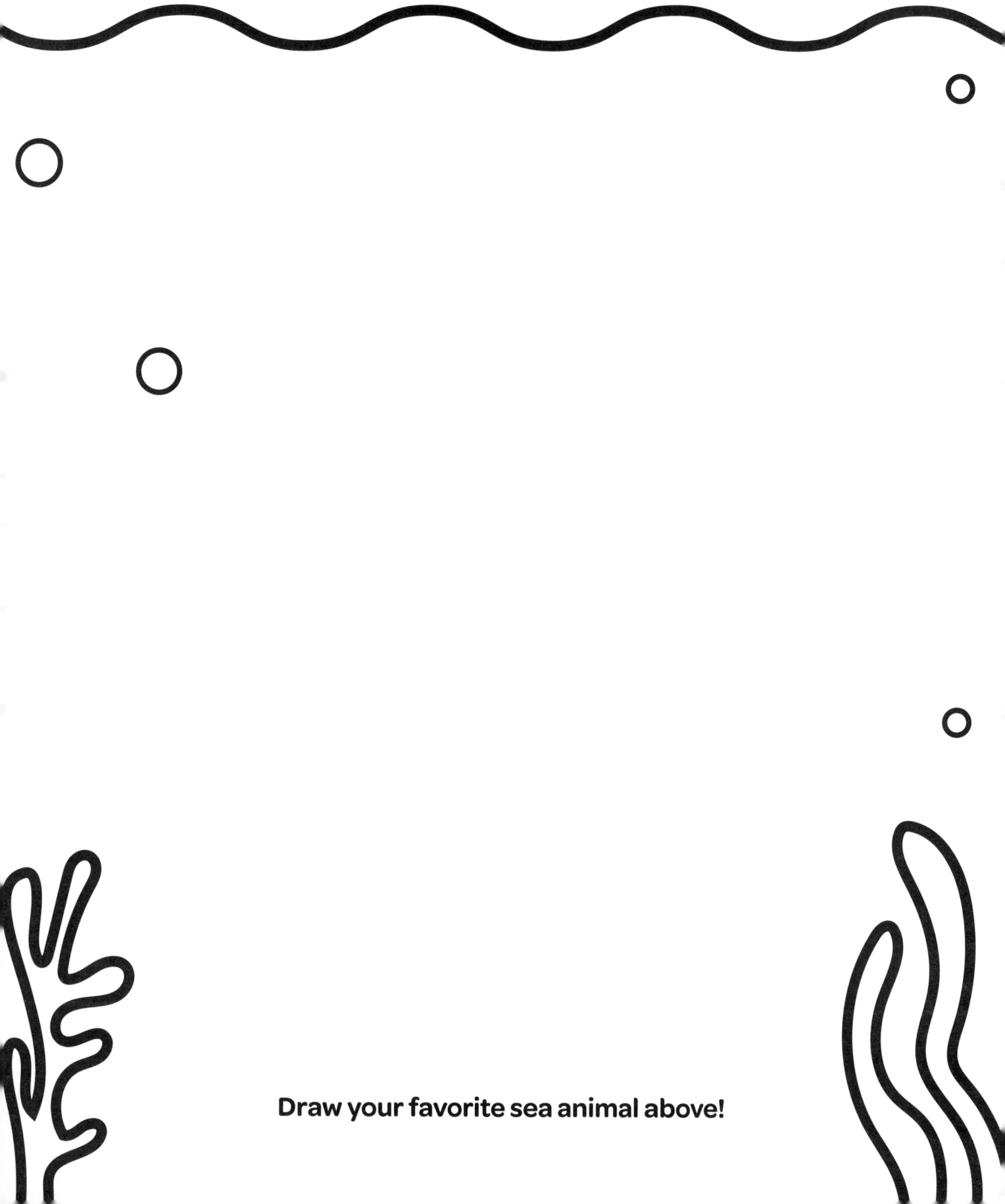

Draw your favorite sea animal above!

Georgia is famous for its peaches!

Let's visit the birthplace of Martin Luther King, Jr. in Atlanta!

Did you know Florida is also called the Sunshine State?

Look at the beautiful magnolia tree! Magnolias represent endurance and long life.

How many alligators can you see in this swamp? Your answer: _____

Welcome to the Everglades! Here, you can find the endangered leatherback turtle.

FL
Can you spot the alligator?

Look!
Someone is paddleboarding.

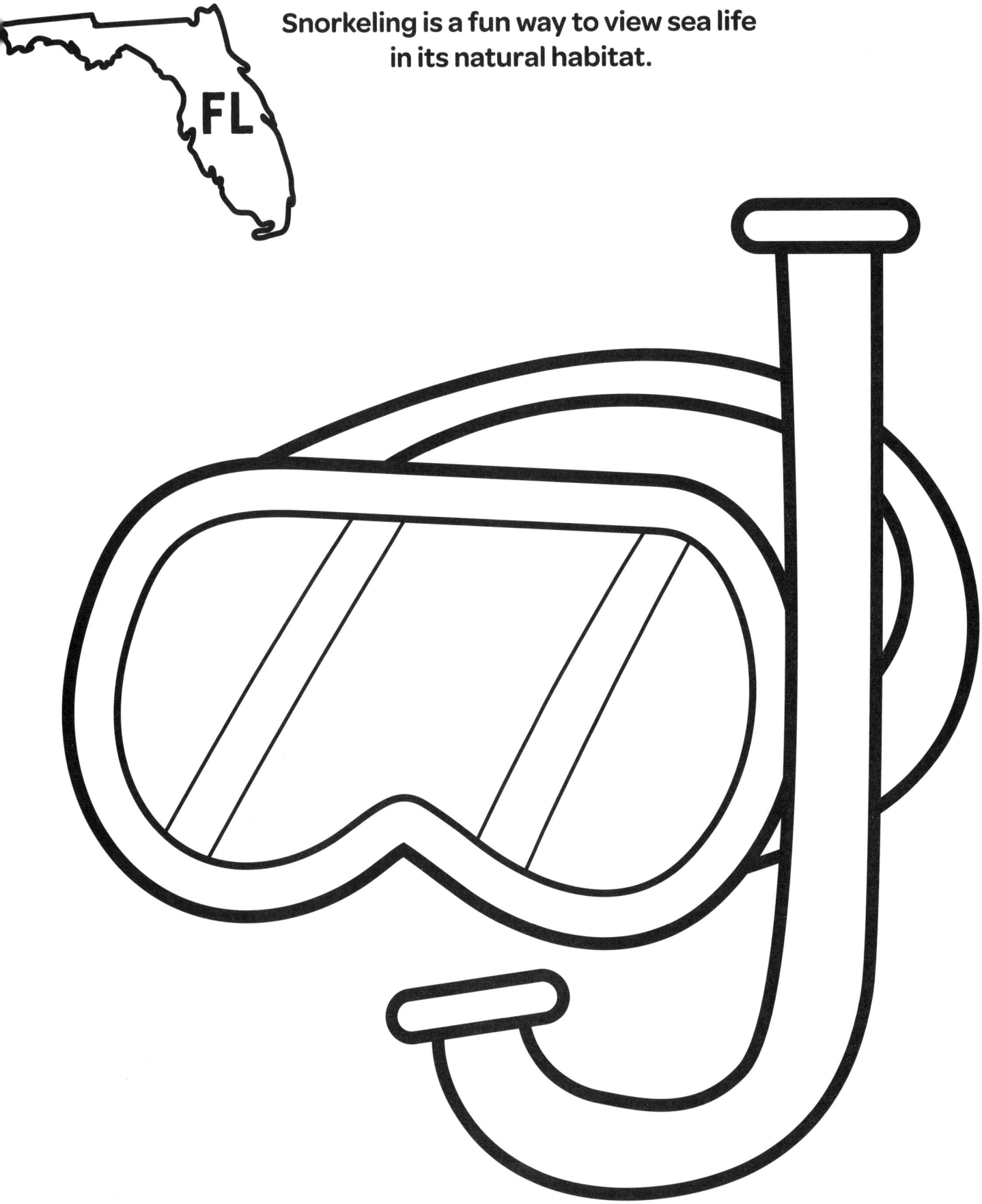

Snorkeling is a fun way to view sea life in its natural habitat.

Ribbit! Ribbit! **Frogs love hopping!**

Flamingos are social birds and live in colonies!

Stop and smell the flowers.
Alabama's state flower is the camellia!

Louisiana is a beautiful state.
Let's go on a shrimp boat tour out of New Orleans!

Connect the dots to see a prickly plant that can be found in hot, dry climates!

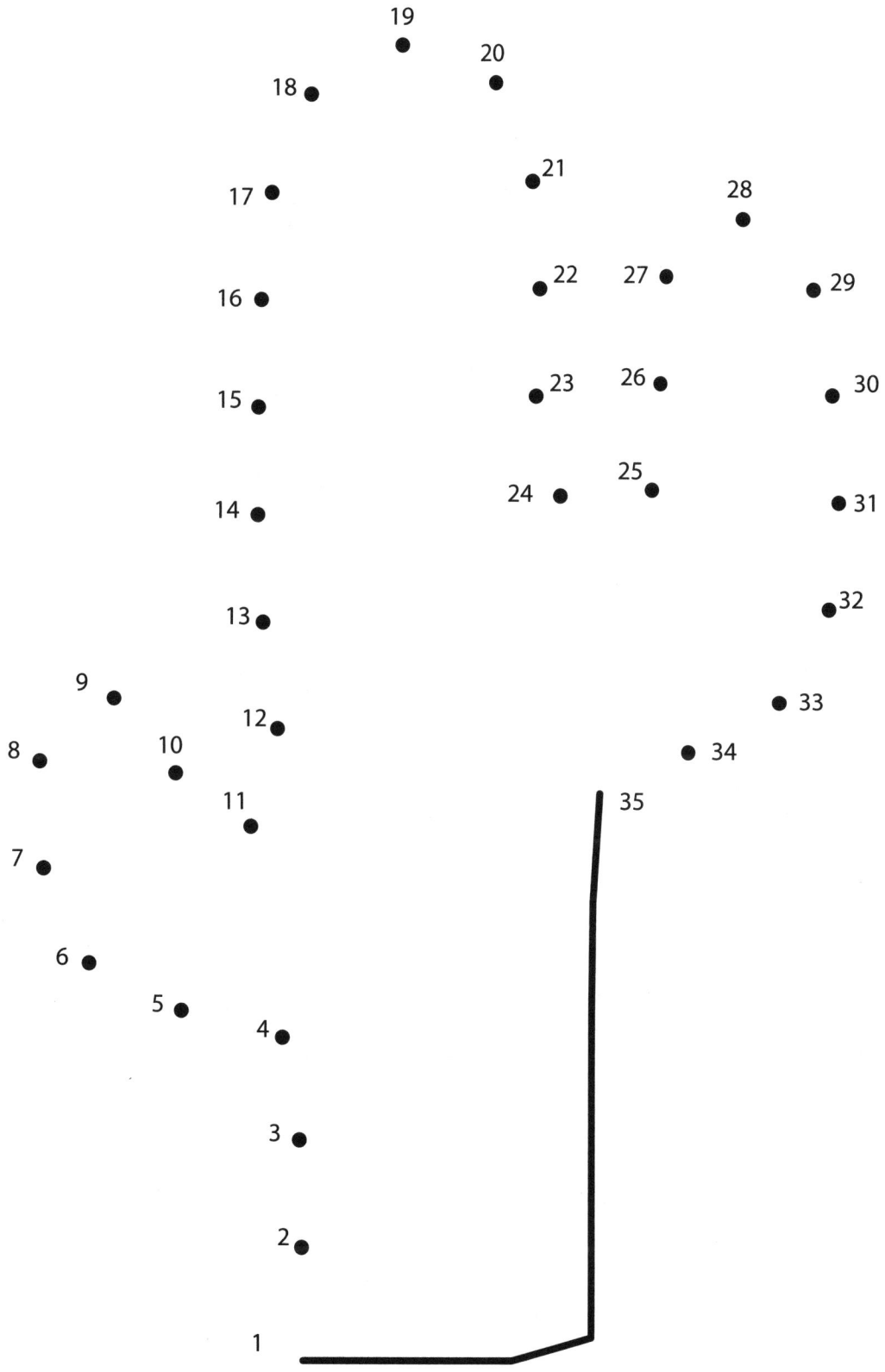

Do you like ducks?
One of Mississippi's state birds is the wood duck!

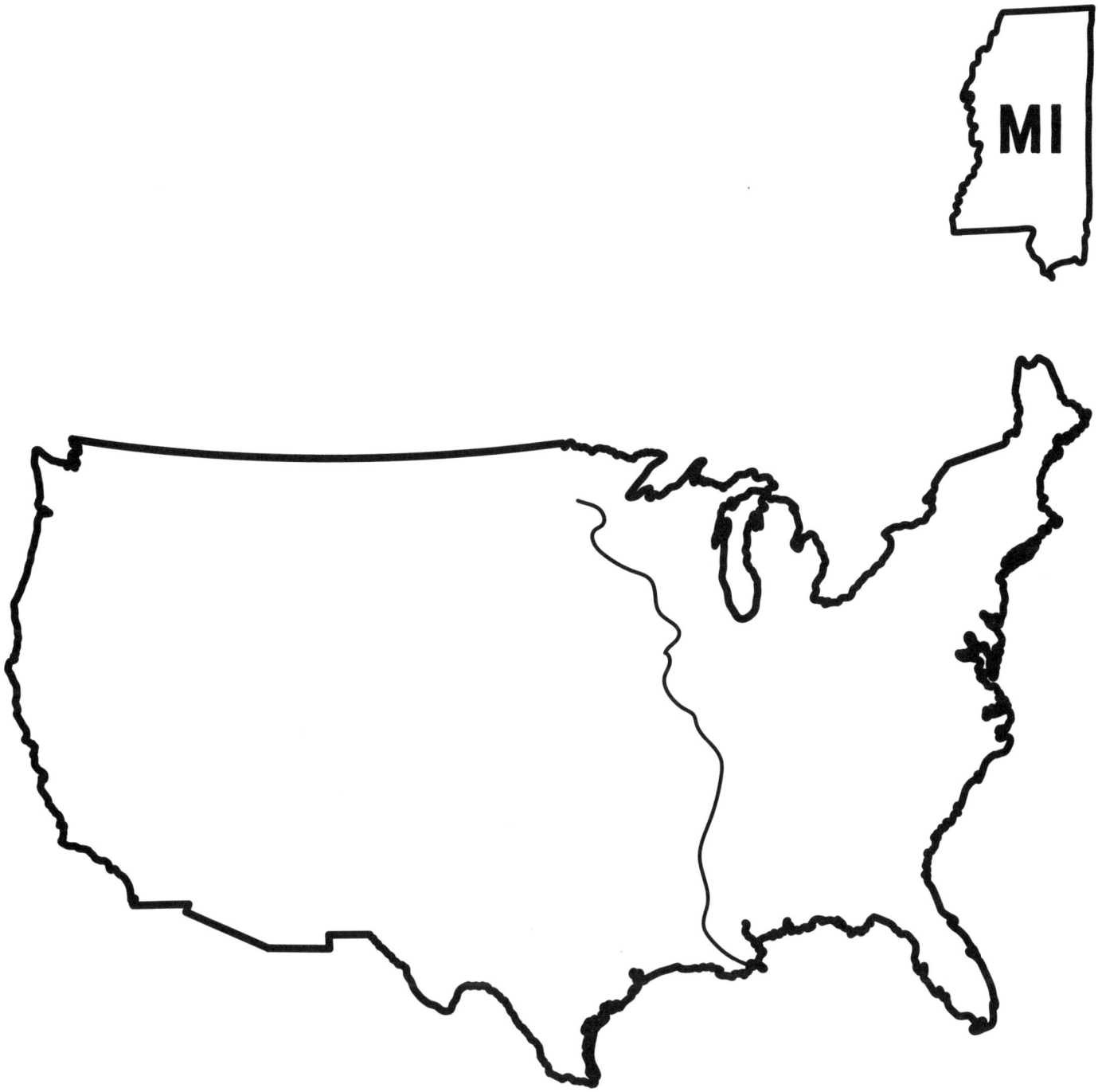

**The Mississippi River is the second-longest river in America.
It runs through ten states!**

Welcome to the Arkansas River Valley!
Let's go fishing.

The white-tailed deer is the state mammal of Arkansas!

The Blue Whale of Catoosa was built in 1972.

Oklahoma's state tree is the redbud!

The Alamo is a historic Spanish mission and the site of the Battle of the Alamo.

Texas is famous for its barbecue!

The Gathering of Nations is held in Albuquerque, New Mexico.
It is the largest powwow in the United States!

Take in the sights of the Taos Pueblo! It's one of the oldest inhabited communities in the U.S.

In Colorado, you can take a tour led by a park ranger in Mesa Verde National Park to see Cliff Palace!

Let's go white water rafting
in the Colorado River!

CO

CO

Cowabunga!
Go sand sledding at the
Great Sand Dunes National Park and Preserve!

Take in the Rocky Mountain scenery at Maroon Bells-Snowmass Wilderness!

NM
How about going on a UFO tour?
Alien sightings have been reported in New Mexico!

The state flower of Arizona is the white blossom of the saguaro—the largest cactus in the United States!

Chuckwallas are members of the iguana family. They can be found in the Arizona desert!

Welcome to the Navajo Nation's
Monument Valley Park!
Its Navajo name is Tsé Bii' Ndzisgaii.

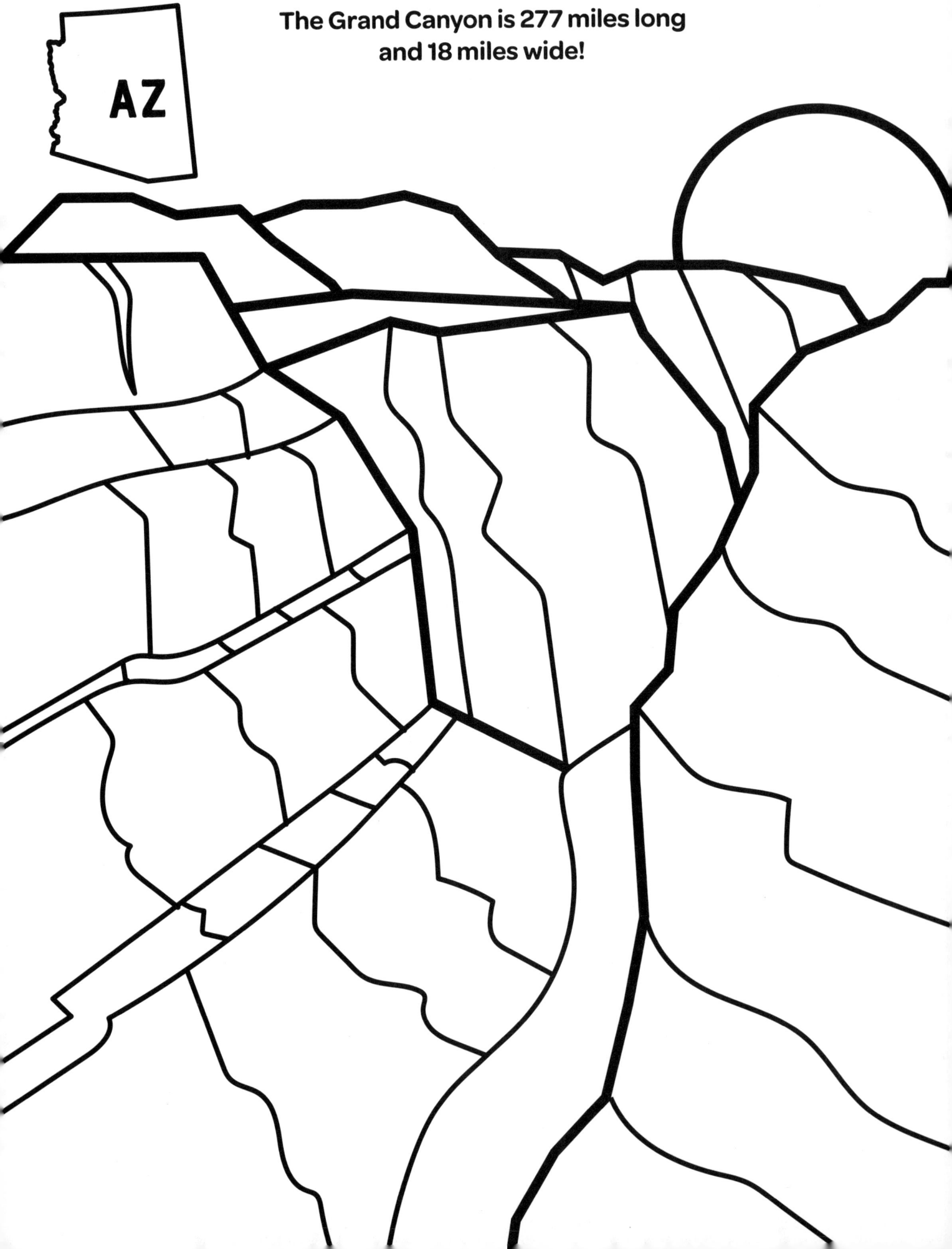

The Grand Canyon is 277 miles long
and 18 miles wide!

The Hoover Dam is used to generate electricity for people in Arizona, Nevada, and California!

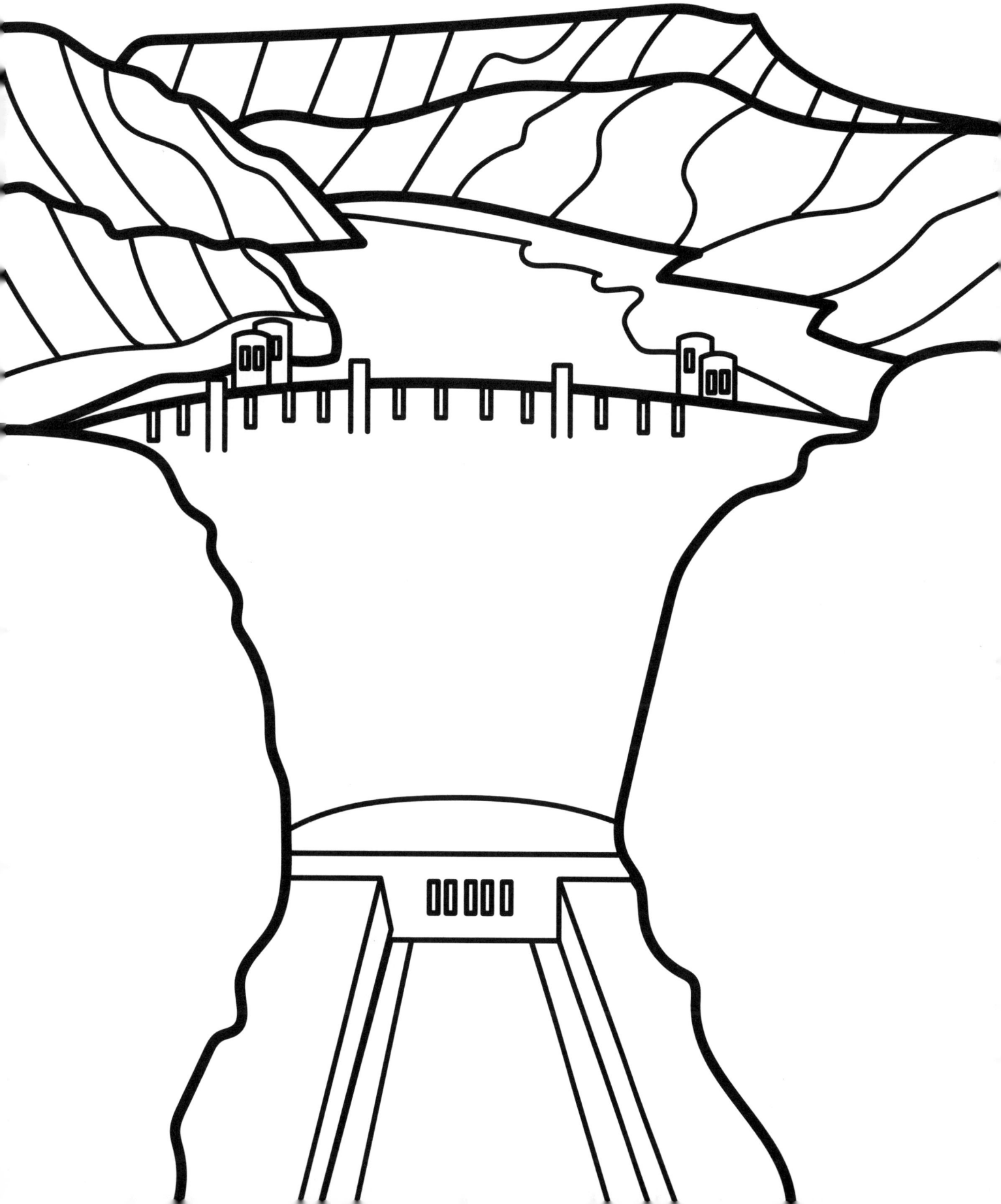

It's relaxing at the beach!

The Santa Monica Pier looks out to the Pacific Ocean on the West Coast!

Look! There's a dolphin!

Surf's up! Decorate the surfboard using different colors.

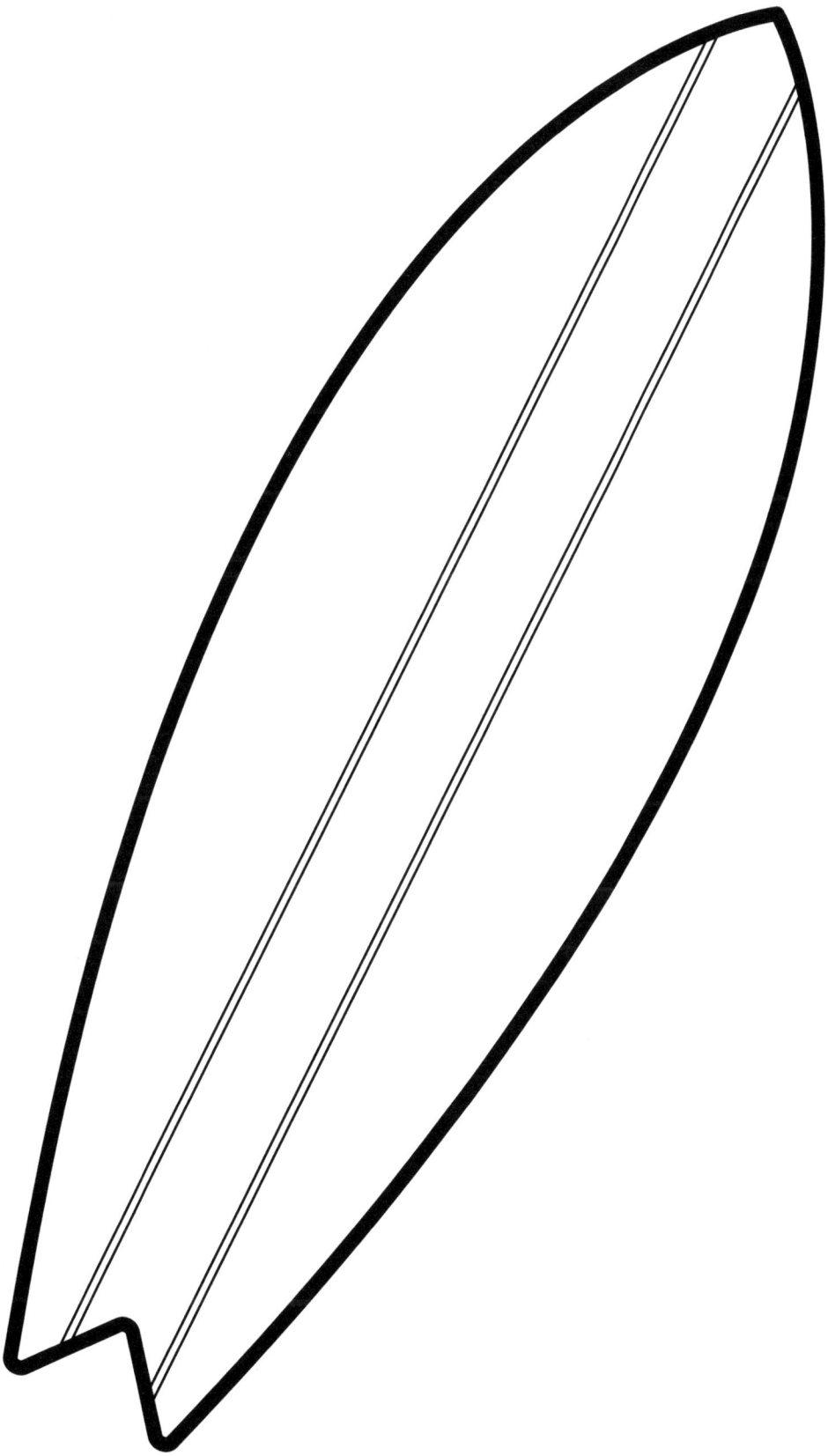

Can you see the Hollywood sign on the hill?

Write your name in this star for the Hollywood Walk of Fame!

How about a spin on the Merry-Go-Round?

Of all the palm trees in Los Angeles, only one species is native to California!

Yosemite Falls is the highest waterfall in Yosemite!

Let's go for a bike ride. Don't forget your helmet!

That large rock formation is called El Capitan.
It's popular amongst rock climbers!

Look—it's the Half Dome!
It's known for its distinct shape.

Let's travel north to see
the Golden Gate Bridge.
It's over a mile and a half long!

Ding! Ding!
Did you know that San Francisco's cable car system is the world's last manually operated cable car system?

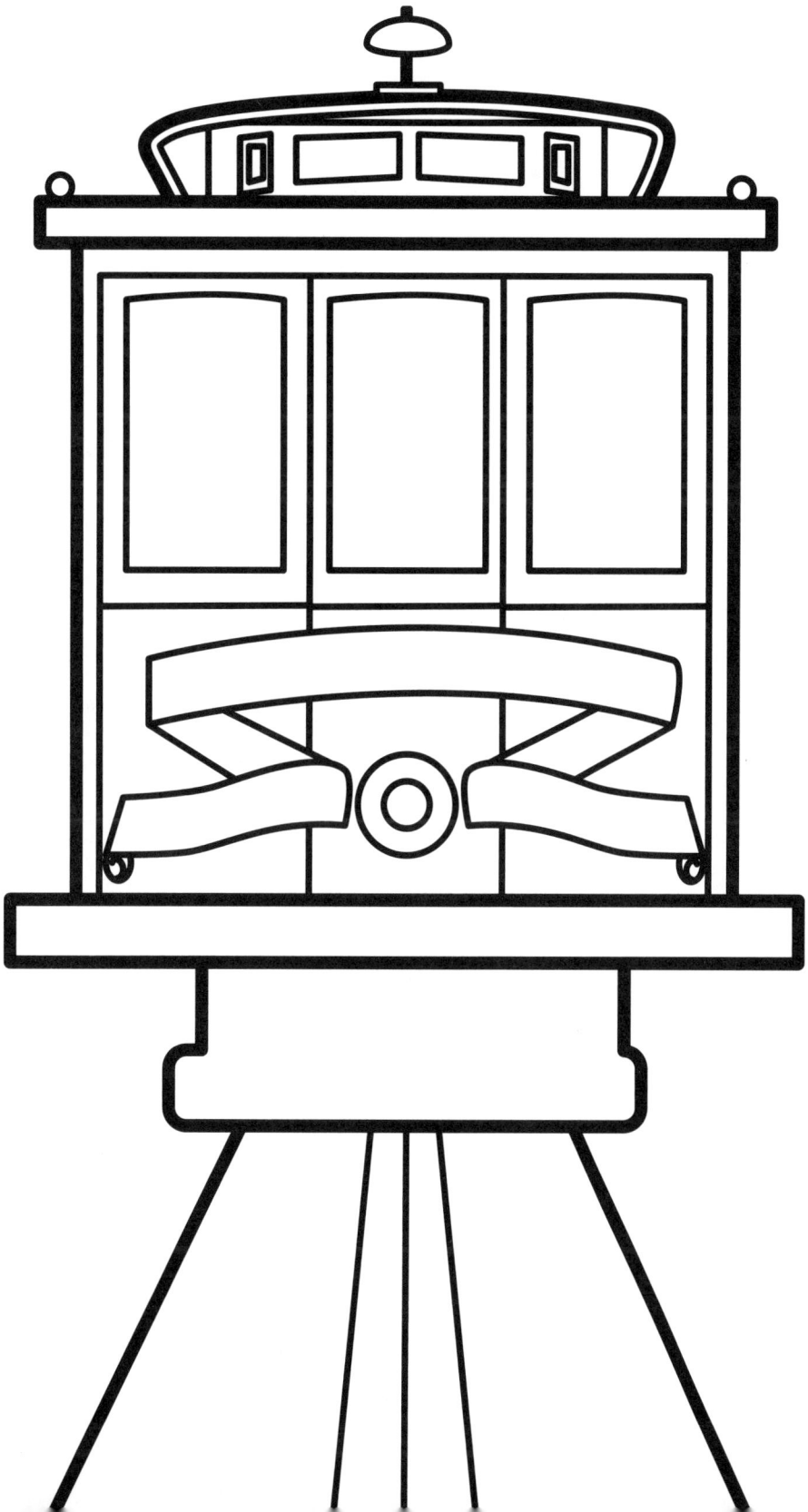

General Sherman Tree is the largest tree in the world. It's a giant sequoia!

How many monarch butterflies can you find?
Your answer:_____

The California poppy is a beautiful flower!

There are 14 different kinds of snakes that can be located in Sequoia National Park!

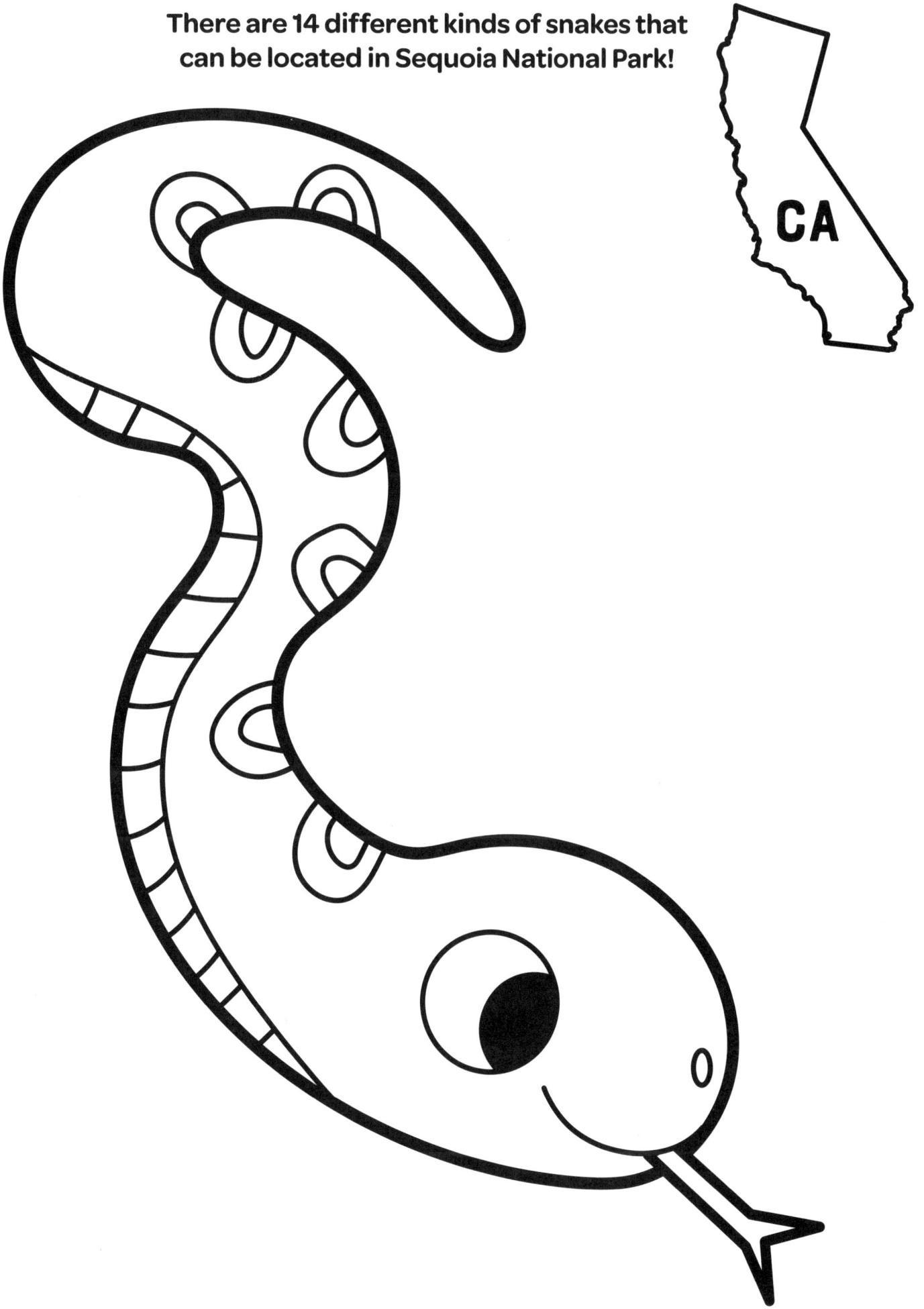

Keep your eyes peeled for the elusive Northern Pygmy-Owl!

Do you recognize this rock?
This landmark, Haystack Rock, is one of the most popular attractions in Oregon!

Crater Lake was formed due to the collapse of volcano Mount Mazama!

Did you know Mount St. Helens is an active volcano in Washington State?

The Space Needle is a 605-foot-tall spire located in Seattle, Washington!

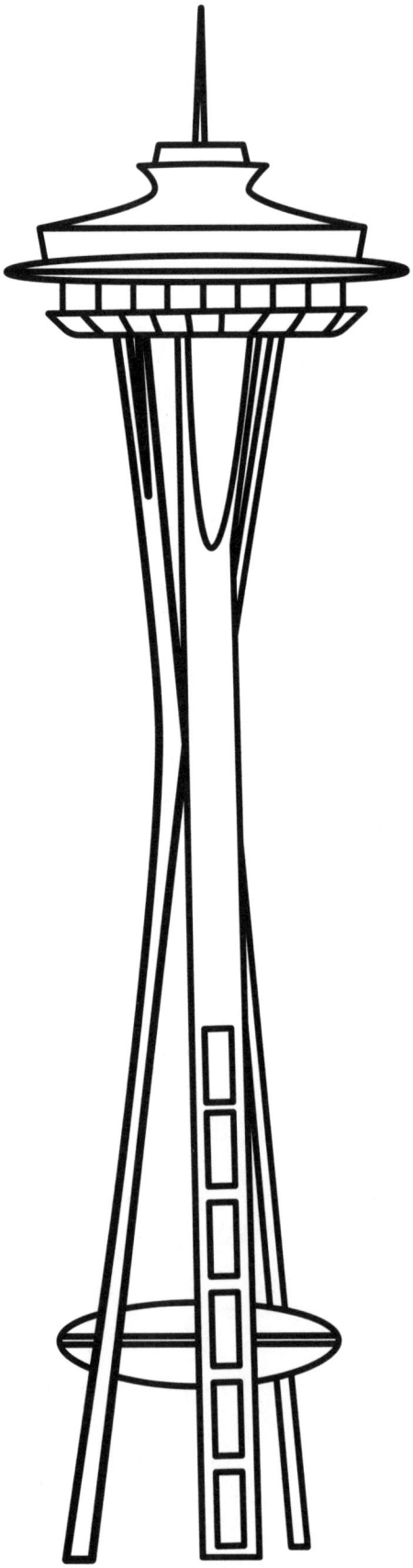

Help the bald eagle get to her nest! Bald eagles are the United States of America's national bird.

Washington's State bird is the American goldfinch!

See that mountain? It's the iconic Washington landmark Mount Rainier. It's a stratovolcano!

It's time to stretch your legs! Let's go on a hike.

What would you want your hiking boots to look like? Color them in!

Don't forget to fill your backpack with what you need!

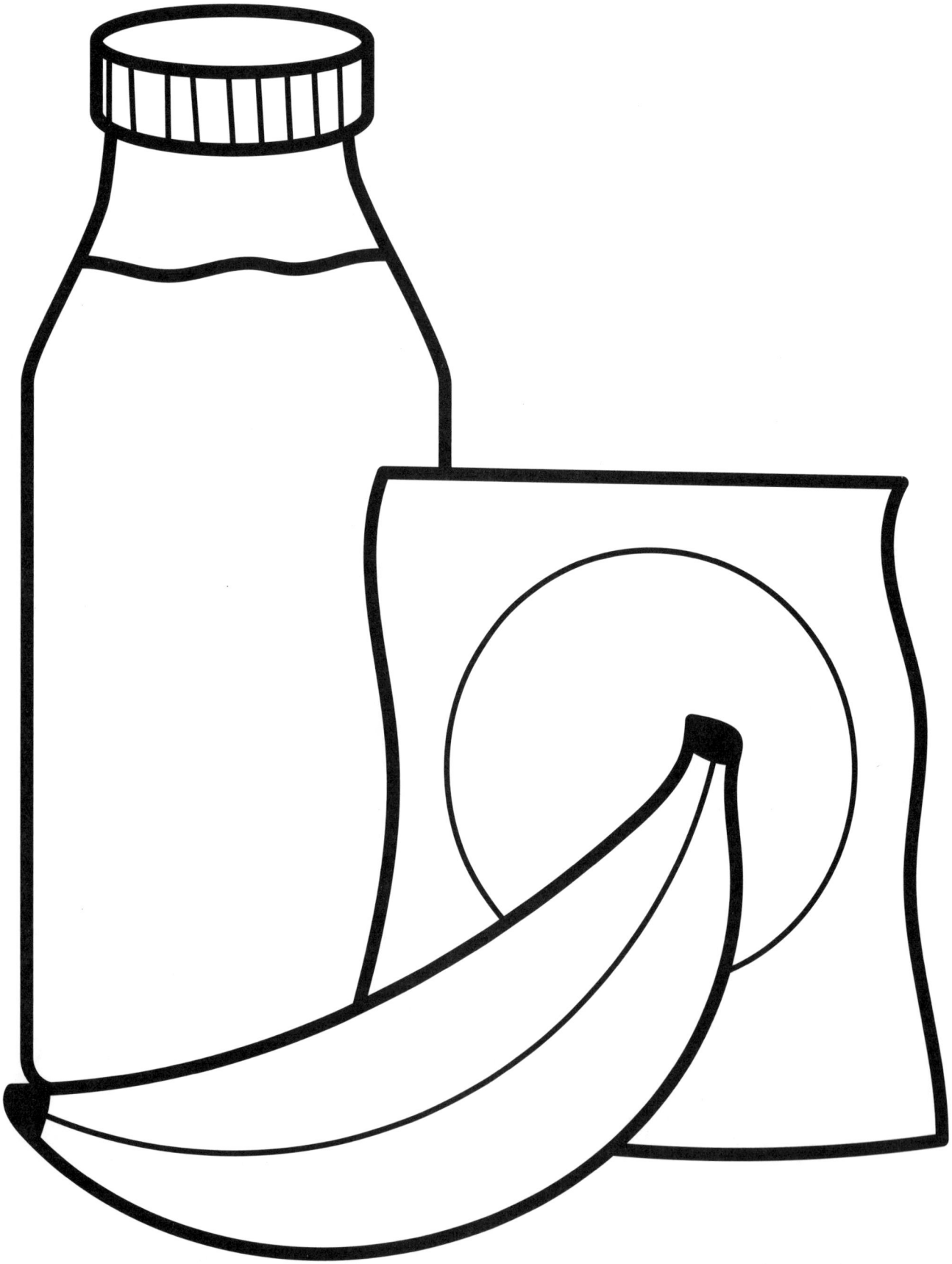

It's the Old Faithful Geyser, one of Yellowstone's most iconic landmarks! A geyser is a vent in earth's surface! It blasts water 130 feet in the air!

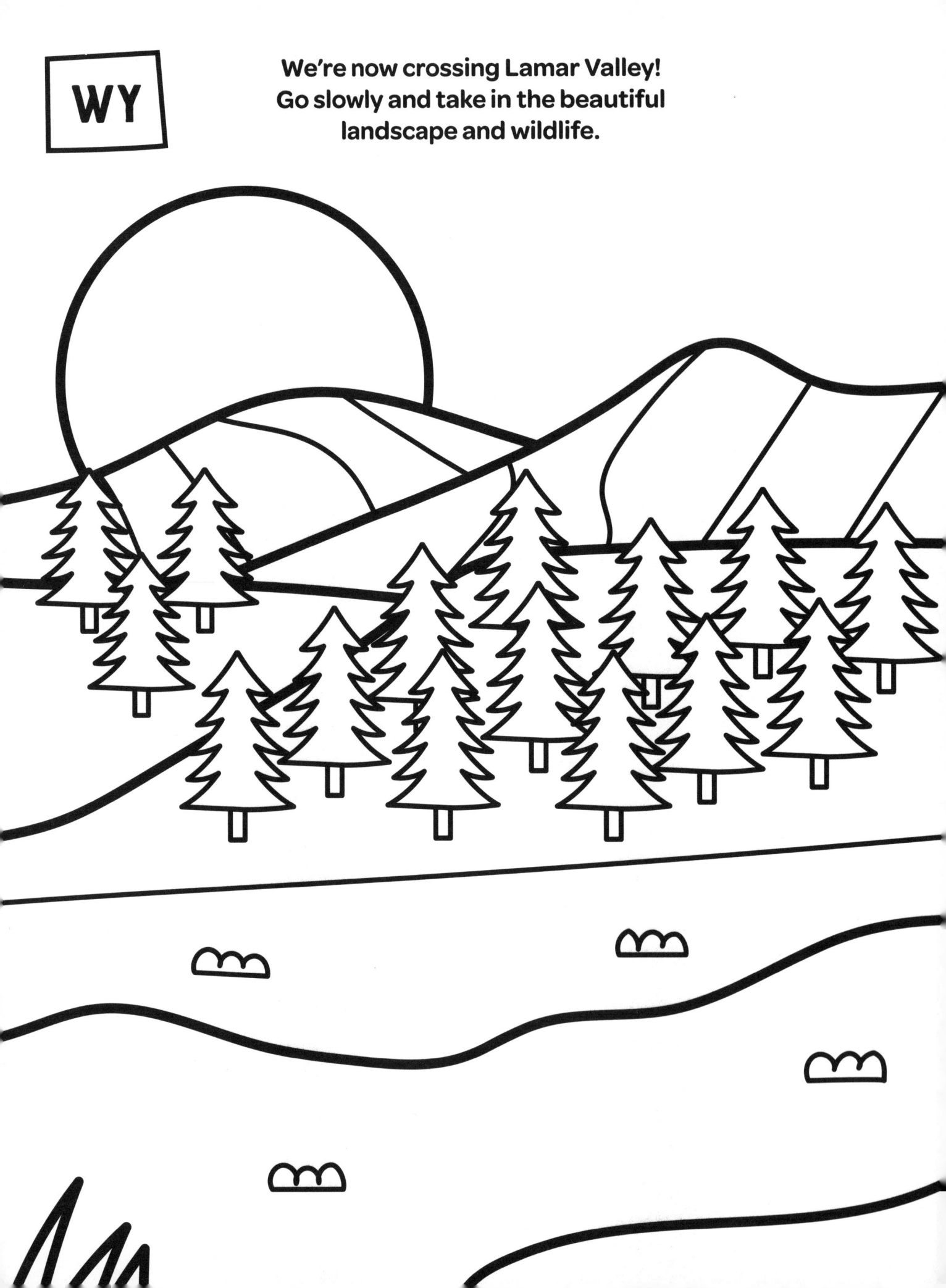
WY
We're now crossing Lamar Valley!
Go slowly and take in the beautiful
landscape and wildlife.

The bison is America's national animal and largest land mammal!

WY

How many bison do you see in the field?
Your answer:_____

Circle the animal that doesn't live in Yellowstone!

Glacier National Park

This grizzly bear is fast!
Did you know they can run up to 30 miles per hour?

Yip! Yip! **Did you know coyotes are good swimmers?**

Circle the tree that is different from the others!

It's a field of wildflowers! Color each flower a different color.

Bald eagles have an average wingspan of 7 feet!

A college football game between the University of North Dakota and Idaho State is called the Potato Bowl USA!

North Dakota is the number-one producer of honey in America!

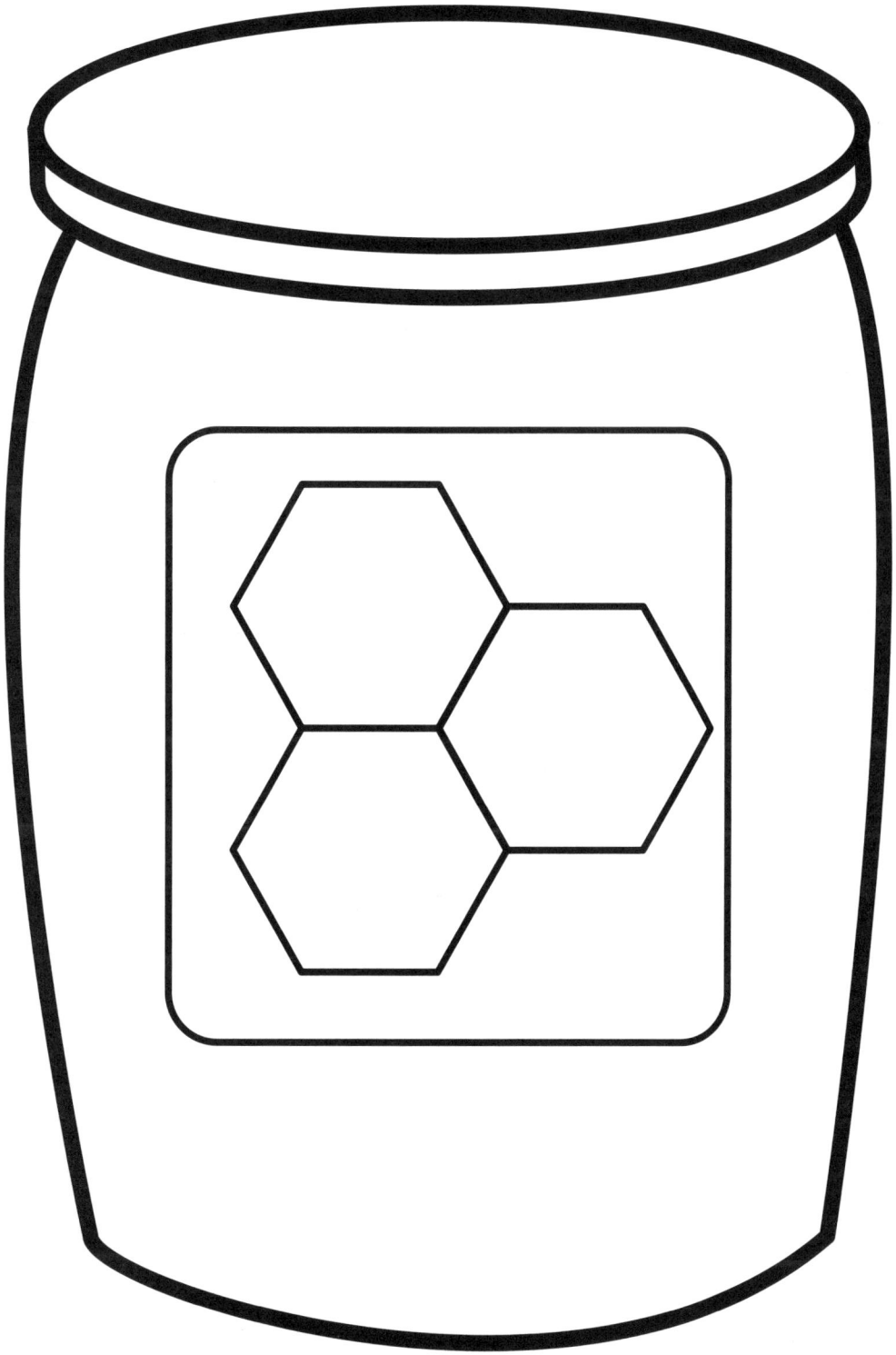

The overlook at the Painted Canyon Visitor Center gives you a great sight of the Badlands!

You can find prairie dogs in the Badlands National Park in South Dakota.

Help the prairie dog get to the grass!

The Mount Rushmore National Memorial carved into the mountains in the Black Hills region of South Dakota depicts U.S. presidents George Washington, Thomas Jefferson, Theodore Roosevelt, and Abraham Lincoln.

South Dakota is home to nine tribes of Indigenous peoples.

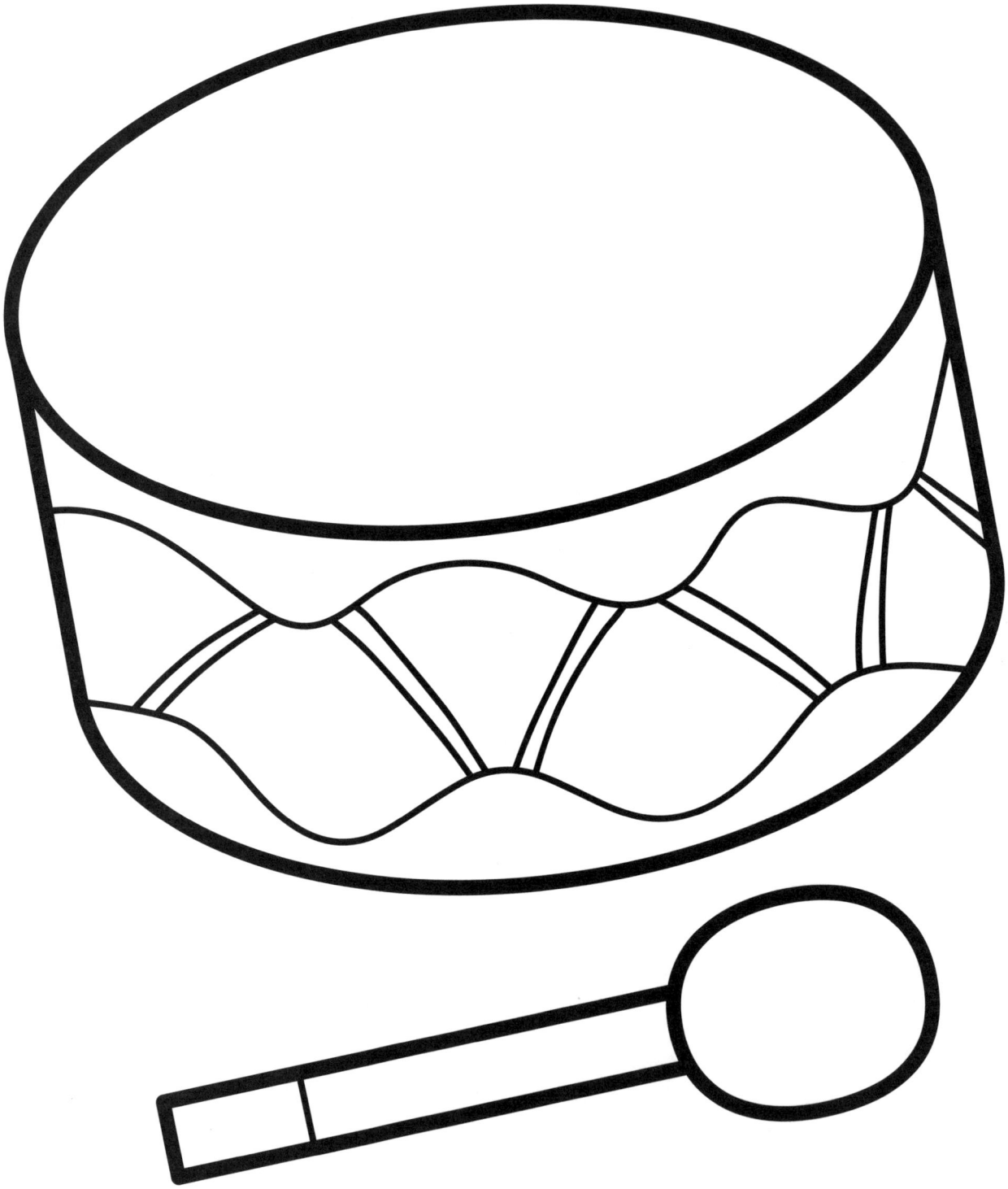

Nebraska's state insect is the honeybee!

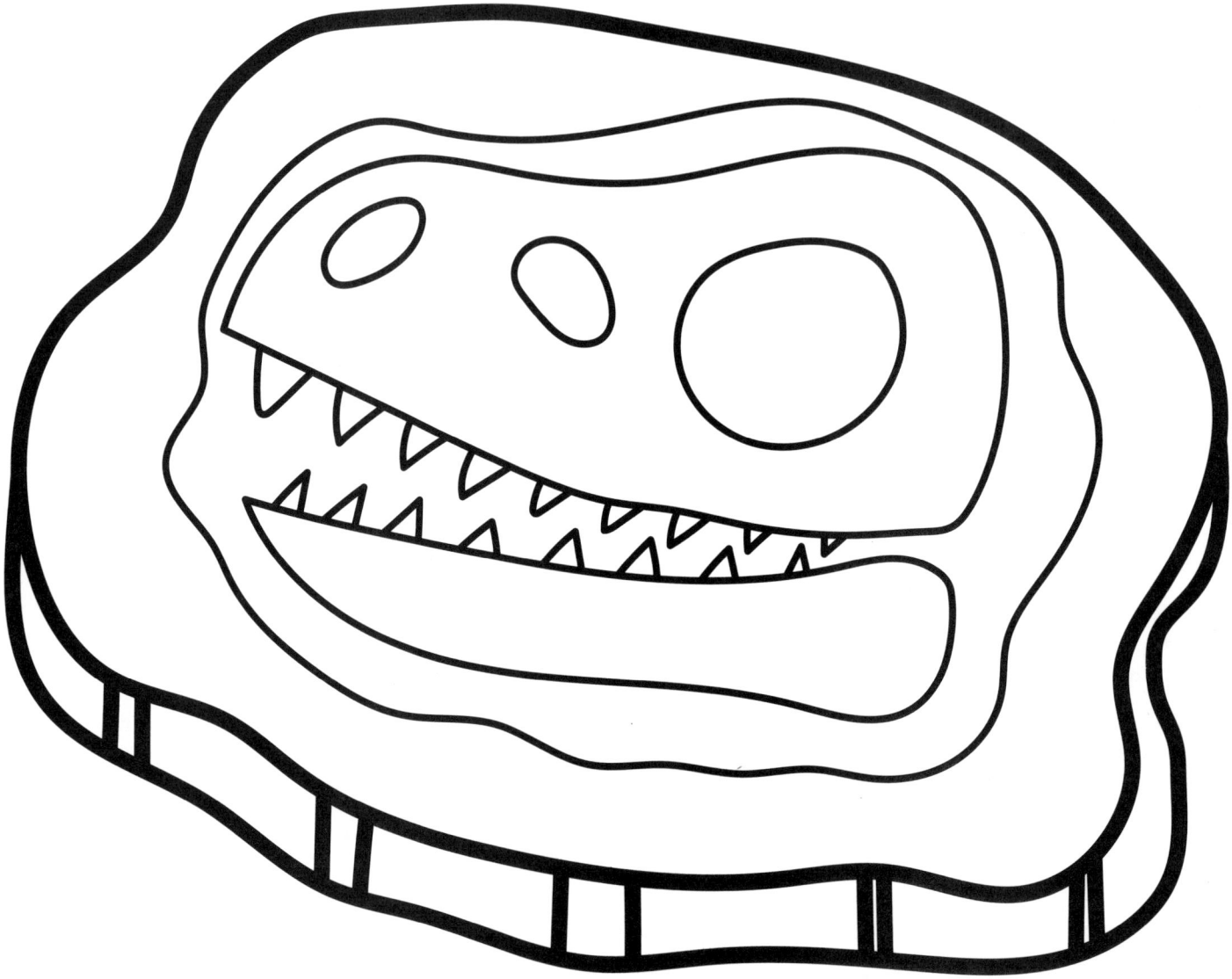

Fossils are awesome! The Ashfall Fossil Beds in Nebraska have fossils of animals who lived over 12 million years ago.

Did you know that Kansas has eight wonders?
One of these is the Monument Rocks.

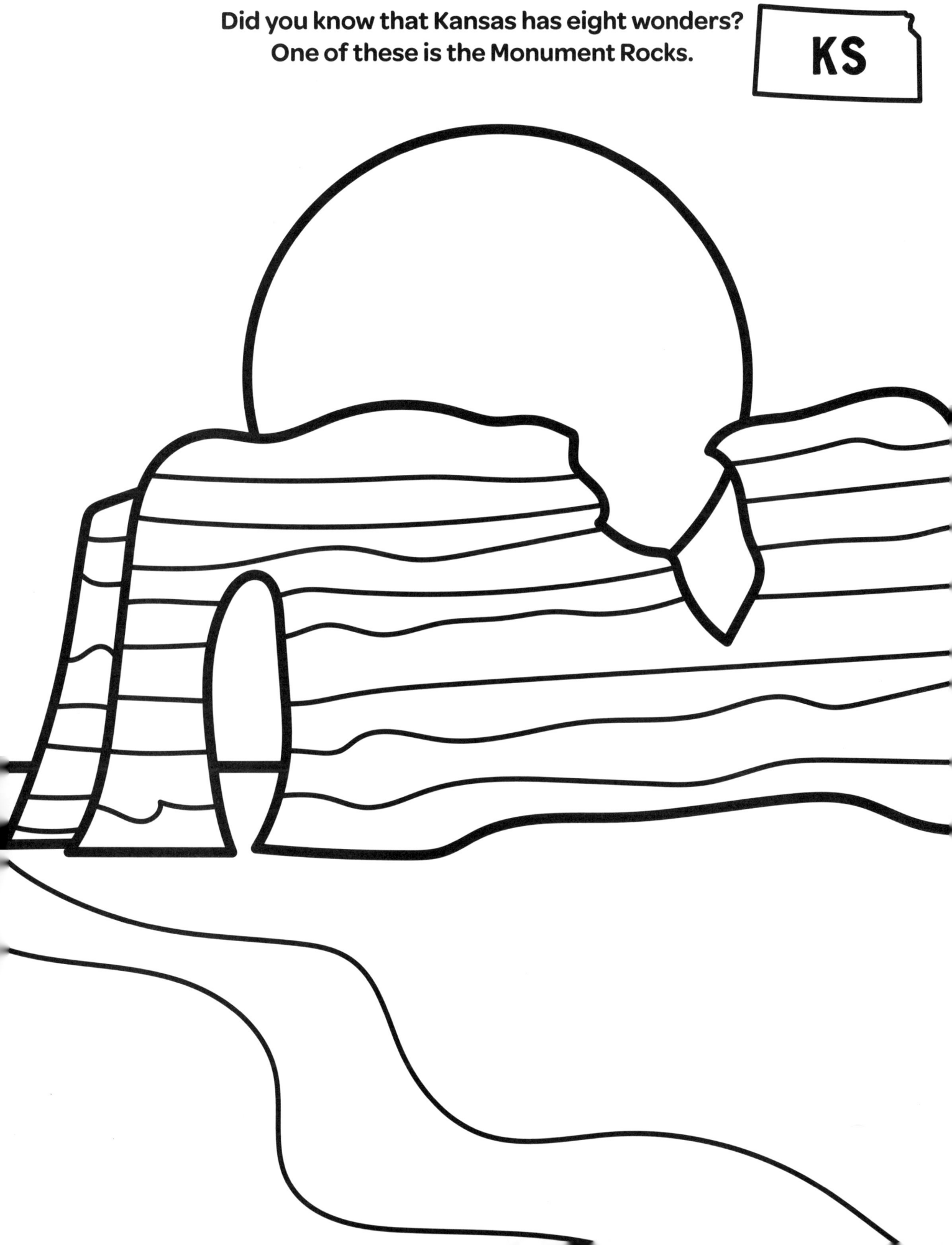

Armadillos can be found in Kansas!
Their name comes from the Spanish work *armado,* which means "*armed.*"

How about stopping to see Missouri's fantastic caverns?

Did you know Missouri is home to the world's second-largest rocking chair?

The Gateway Arch is the world's tallest arch!

There's plenty of wildlife to see in Lone Elk Park!

Chirp! Chirp!
Did you know crickets listen with tiny ears they have on their legs ?

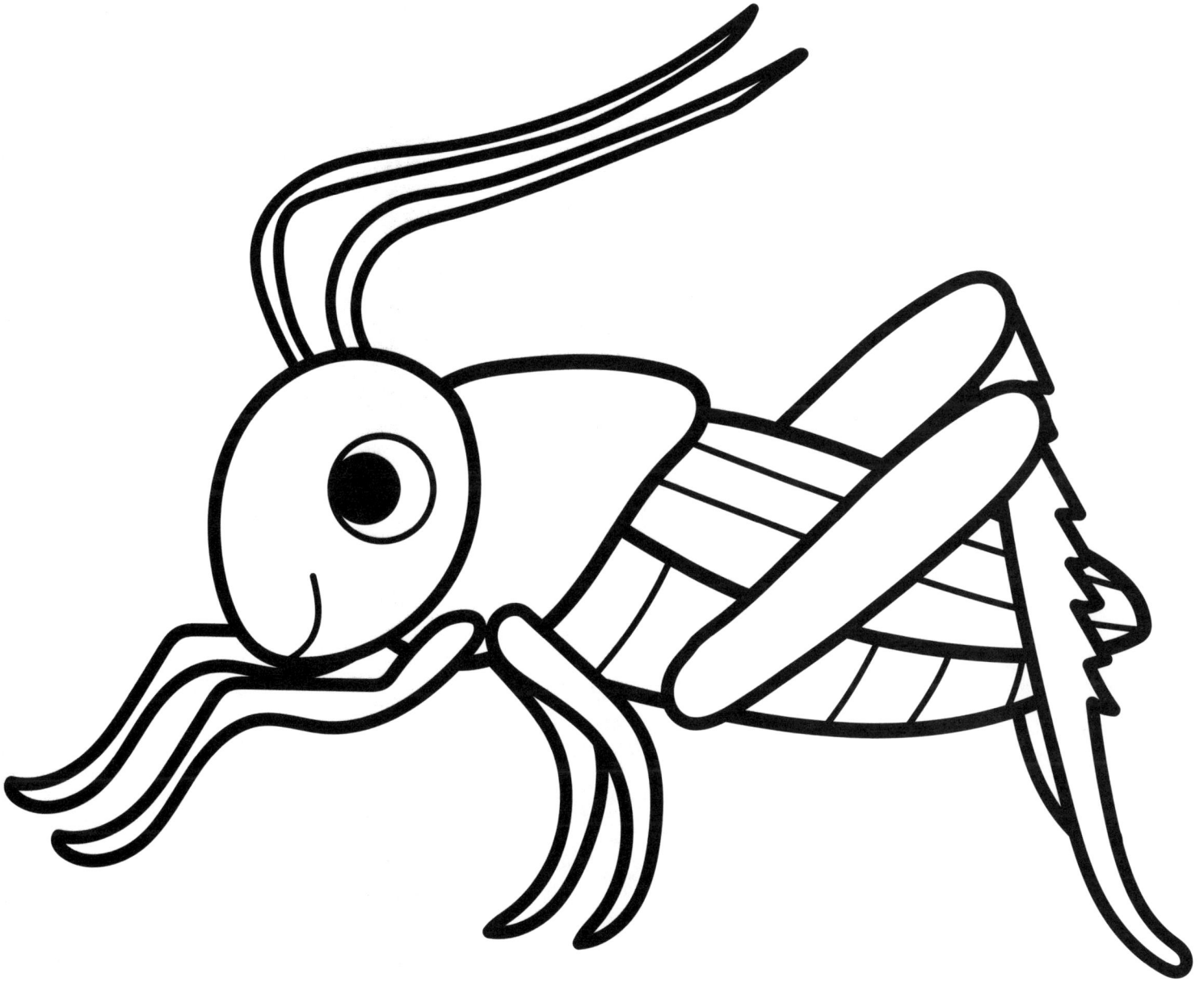

Have you heard of Elwood?
He's the world's tallest concrete gnome!
He can be found in Iowa.

Iowa has nine types of bats!
This one is a little brown bat.

Minnesota is home to Superior National Forest and the International Wolf Center.

Wisconsin has a lot of dairy farming!

Do you like to go camping? Color the picture in to make your perfect tent!

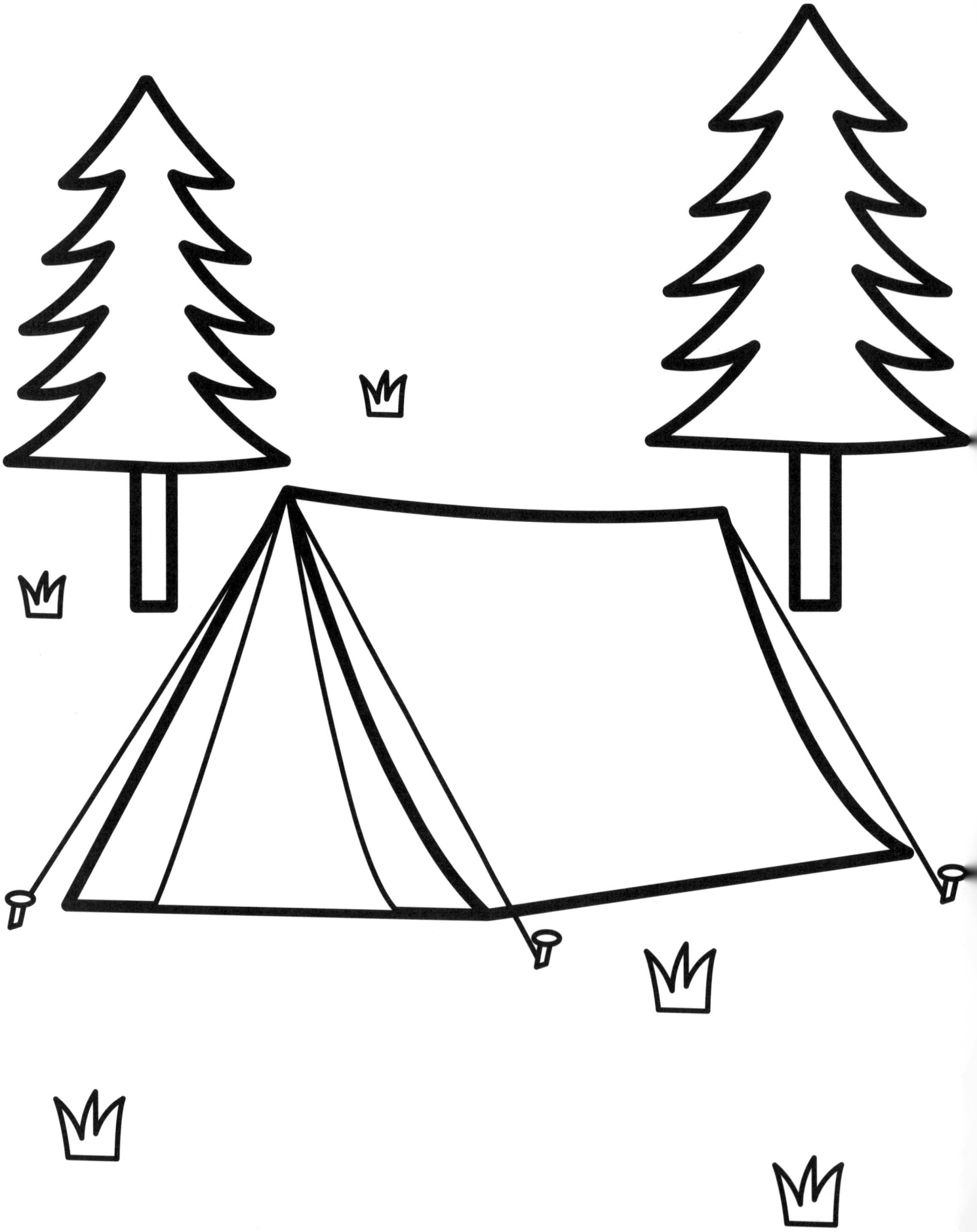

Can you match each animal to its name?

Fox

Snake

Owl

Pee-yew! **That skunk is cute, but smelly!**

Check the car's gas gauge. Uh, oh. It's on E!

Help the car get to the gas station!

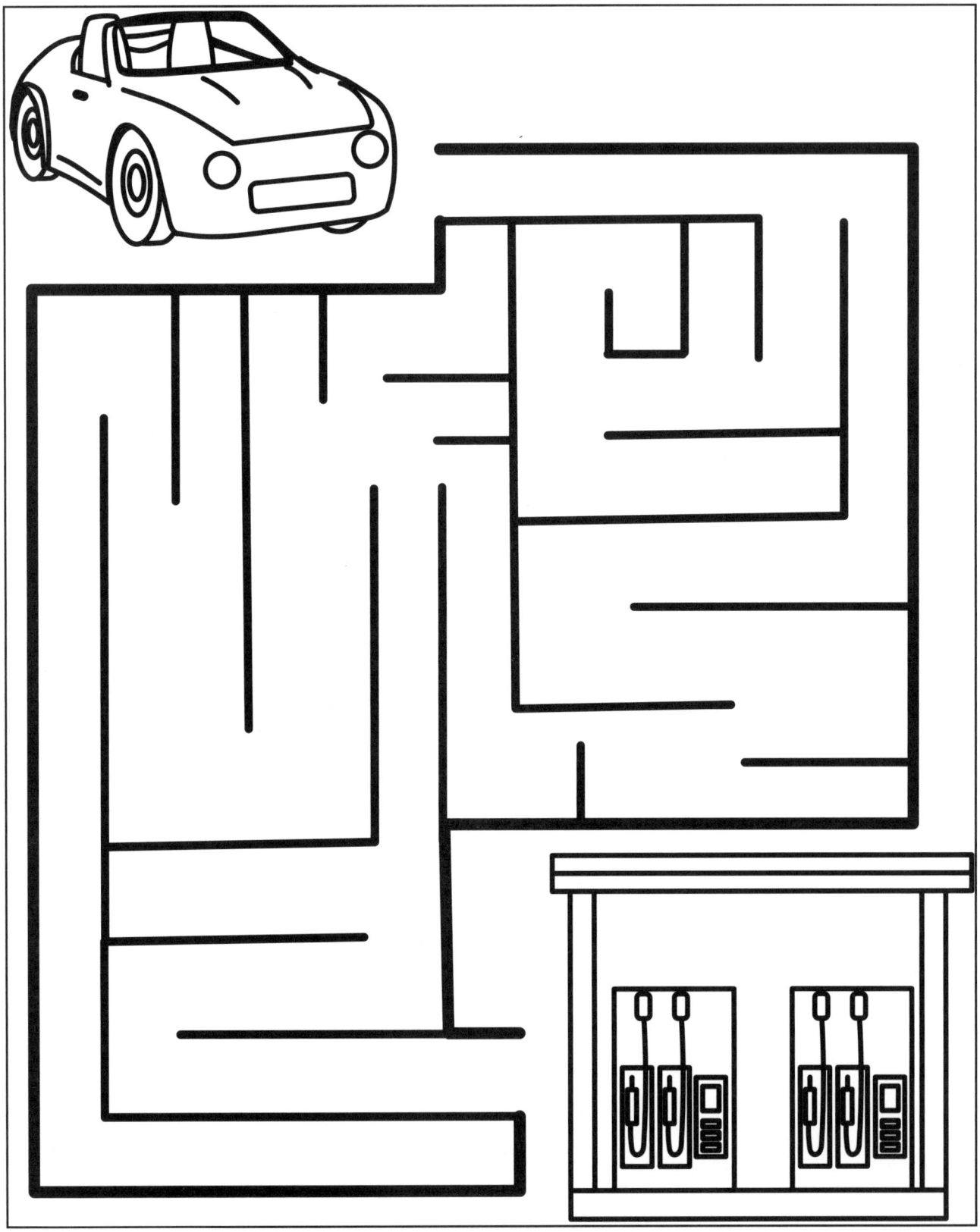

Whew, that was close! Let's get back on the road.

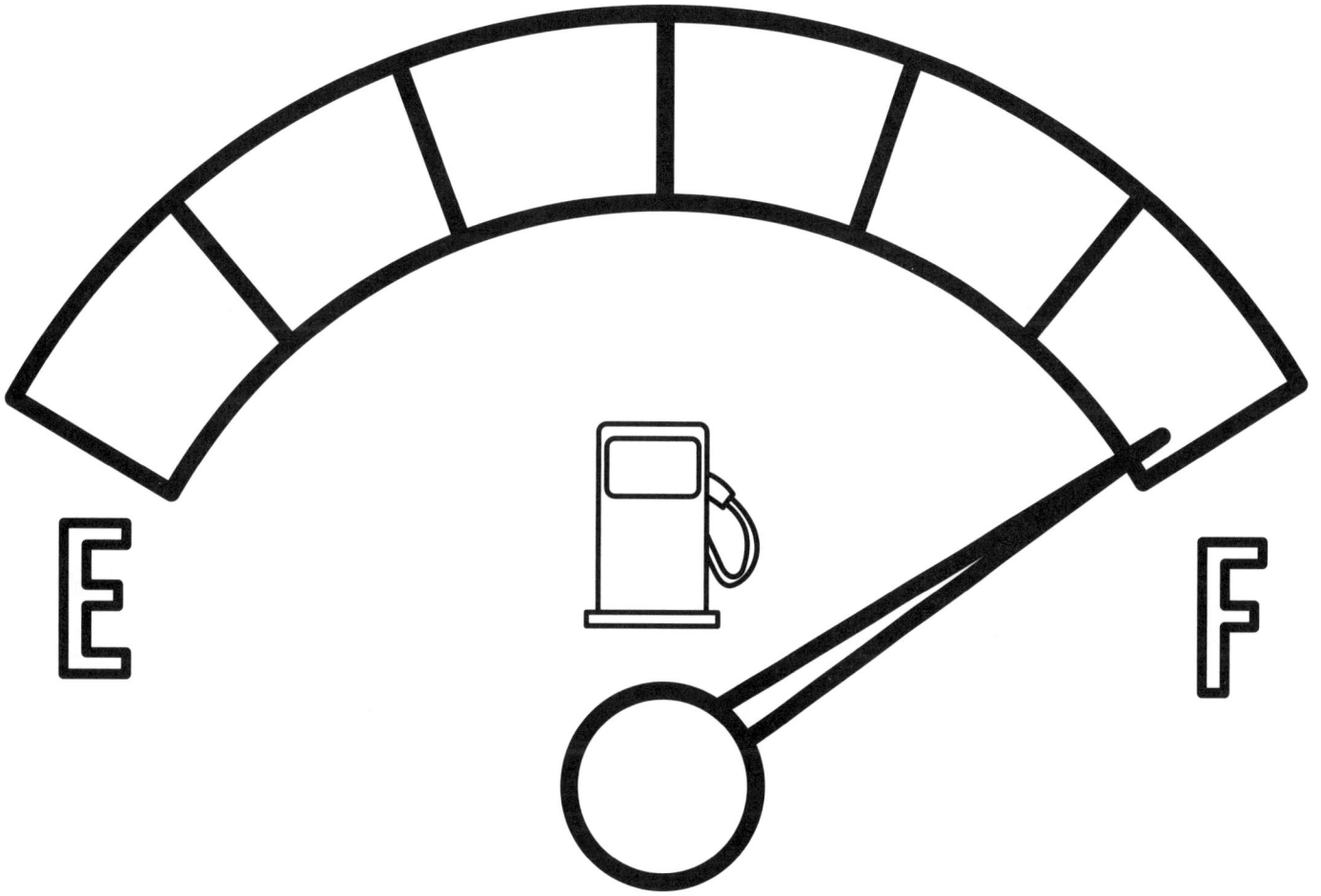

It seems there's some roadwork up ahead, so let's take a detour!

Fill in this photo of your favorite part of the trip!

Circle the truck that has the most wheels!

The highway sure looks busy!

You've made it back home! Fill in the sign with your home state or town.

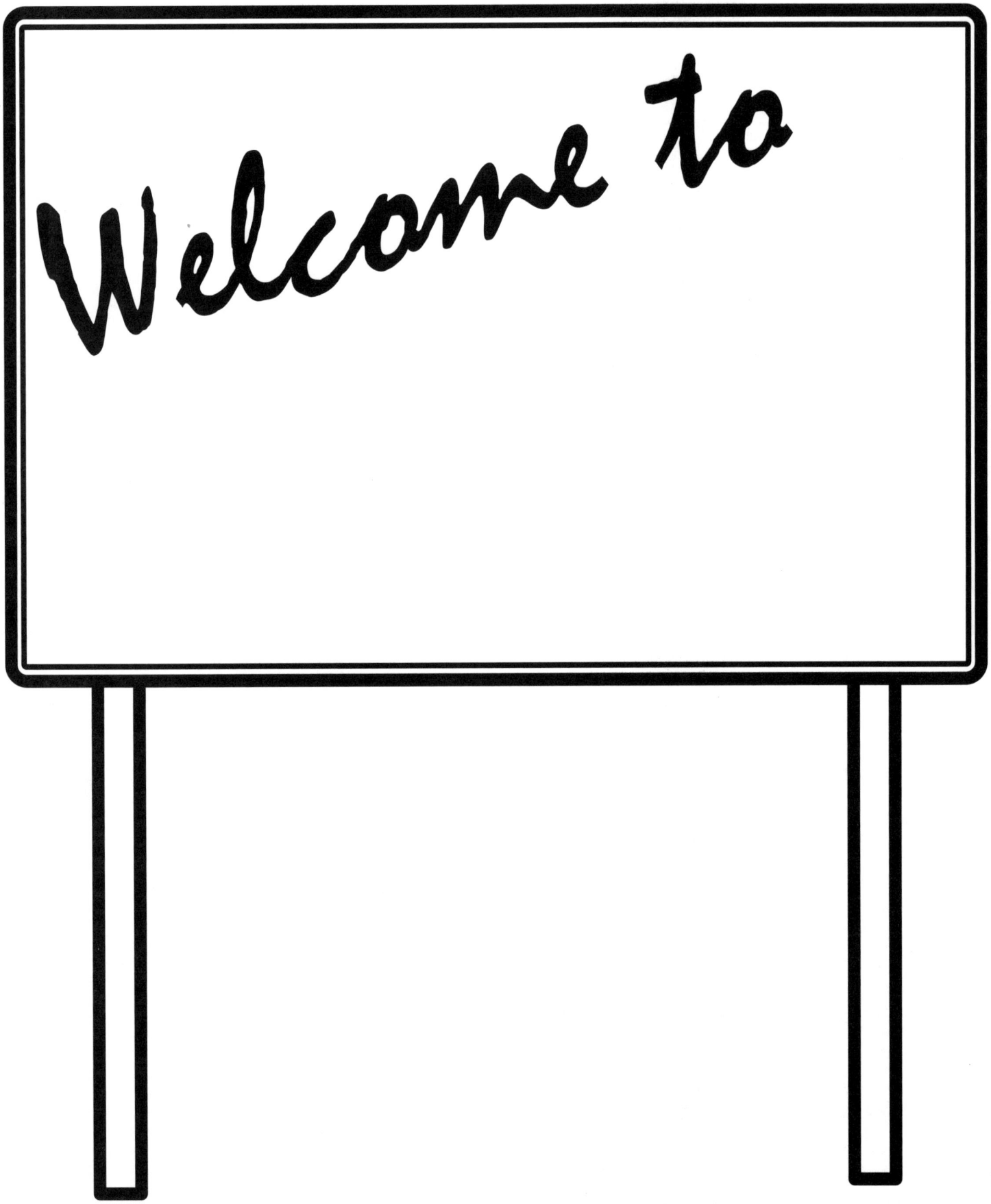

Hope you had a wheel-y nice time!

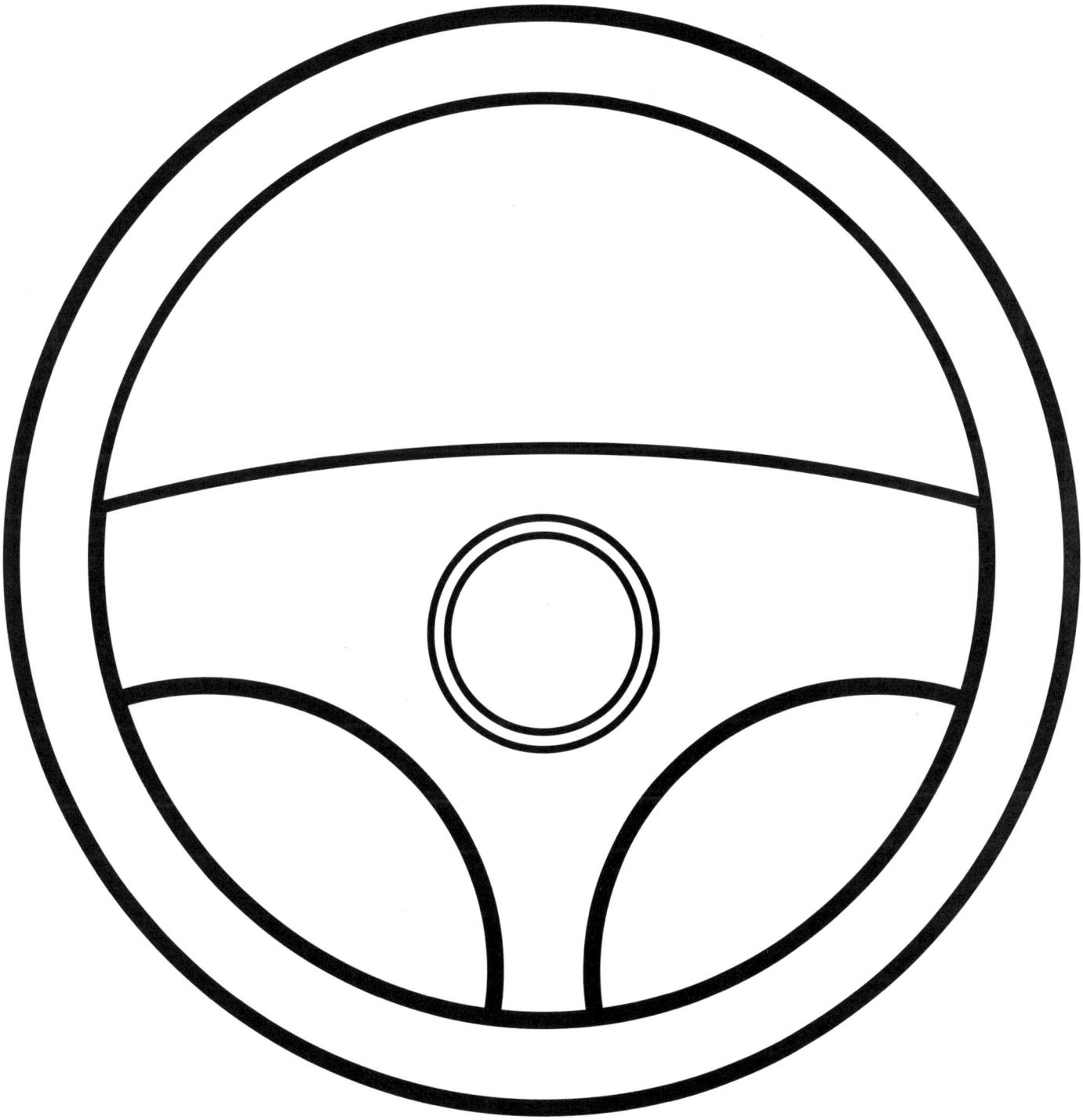

Here's a look at where we've been.